▶ **Adoption**

DOI: 10.1057/9781137333919

Other Palgrave Pivot titles

Maria-Ionela Neagu: **Decoding Political Discourse: Conceptual Metaphors and Argumentation**

Ralf Emmers: **Resource Management and Contested Territories in East Asia**

Niranjan Ramakrishnan: **Reading Gandhi in the Twenty-First Century**

Joel Gwynne: **Erotic Memoirs and Postfeminism: The Politics of Pleasure**

Ira Nadel: **Modernism's Second Act: A Cultural Narrative**

Andy Sumner and Richard Mallett: **The Future of Foreign Aid: Development Cooperation and the New Geography of Global Poverty**

Tariq Mukhimer: **Hamas Rule in Gaza: Human Rights under Constraint**

Khen Lampert: **Meritocratic Education and Social Worthlessness**

G. Douglas Atkins: **Swift's Satires on Modernism: Battlegrounds of Reading and Writing**

David Schultz: **American Politics in the Age of Ignorance: Why Lawmakers Choose Belief over Research**

G. Douglas Atkins: **T.S. Eliot Materialized: Literal Meaning and Embodied Truth**

Martin Barker: **Live To Your Local Cinema: The Remarkable Rise of Livecasting**

Michael Bennett: **Narrating the Past through Theatre: Four Crucial Texts**

Arthur Asa Berger: **Media, Myth, and Society**

Hamid Dabashi: **Being a Muslim in the World**

David Elliott: **Fukushima: Impacts and Implications**

Milton J. Esman: **The Emerging American Garrison State**

Kelly Forrest: **Moments, Attachment and Formations of Selfhood: Dancing with Now**

Steve Fuller: **Preparing for Life in Humanity 2.0**

Ioannis N. Grigoriadis: **Instilling Religion in Greek and Turkish Nationalism: A "Sacred Synthesis"**

Jonathan Hart: **Textual Imitation: Making and Seeing in Literature**

Akira Iriye: **Global and Transnational History: The Past, Present, and Future**

Mikael Klintman: **Citizen-Consumers and Evolutionary Theory: Reducing Environmental Harm through Our Social Motivation**

Helen Jefferson Lenskyj: **Gender Politics and the Olympic Industry**

Christos Lynteris: **The Spirit of Selflessness in Maoist China: Socialist Medicine and the New Man**

Ekpen James Omonbude: **Cross-border Oil and Gas Pipelines and the Role of the Transit Country: Economics, Challenges, and Solutions**

William F. Pinar: **Curriculum Studies in the United States: Present Circumstances, Intellectual Histories**

Henry Rosemont, Jr.: **A Reader's Companion to the Confucian** *Analects*

Kazuhiko Togo (*editor*): **Japan and Reconciliation in Post-war Asia: The Murayama Statement and Its Implications**

Joel Wainwright: **Geopiracy: Oaxaca, Militant Empiricism, and Geographical Thought**

Kath Woodward: **Sporting Times**

DOI: 10.1057/9781137333919

palgrave▸**pivot**

Adoption: A Brief Social and Cultural History

Peter Conn

palgrave
macmillan

DOI: 10.1057/9781137333919

First published in 2013 by
PALGRAVE MACMILLAN®
in the United States—a division of St. Martin's Press LLC,
175 Fifth Avenue, New York, NY 10010.

Where this book is distributed in the UK, Europe and the rest of the world,
this is by Palgrave Macmillan, a division of Macmillan Publishers Limited,
registered in England, company number 785998, of Houndmills,
Basingstoke, Hampshire RG21 6XS.

Palgrave Macmillan is the global academic imprint of the above companies
and has companies and representatives throughout the world.

Palgrave® and Macmillan® are registered trademarks in the United States,
the United Kingdom, Europe and other countries.

ISBN: 978-1-137-33390-2   EPUB
ISBN: 978-1-137-33391-9   PDF
ISBN: 978-1-137-33220-2   Hardback

Library of Congress Cataloging-in-Publication Data is available from the
Library of Congress.

A catalogue record of the book is available from the British Library.

First edition: 2013

www.palgrave.com/pivot

DOI: 10.1057/9781137333919

This is Jennifer's book.

DOI: 10.1057/9781137333919

Contents

DOI: 10.1057/9781137333919

Prologue: What Is Adoption?

I don't recall when it started, but I first noticed it about thirty years ago, on a sunny summer afternoon at the Philadelphia Zoo. The cast of characters on this occasion included my wife, Terry, and I, and our four children: in chronological order from youngest to oldest, Jennifer, Alison, David, and Steven. Jennifer, who was about nine at the time, is our adopted Korean daughter. As the six of us walked from one section of the zoo to another, we noticed that several of the enclosures featured newly installed signs inviting visitors to "adopt an animal." I cannot remember just which animals were available for adoption, but I'd guess that polar bears and monkeys and lions would have been likely candidates. I had never seen such an appeal before.

"Adopt an animal," said Jennifer in a hushed and puzzled voice, reading aloud from one of the signs. She read it several times, then turned to her older brothers and sister for information and advice. Terry and I watched, unsure whether to be amused or just confused. Being parents has usually confused us, so we chose confusion as our initial response.

"Adopt an animal," she said again. Does this mean, Jennifer wanted to know, that we could take an animal home with us? Would it become part of our family? Where would it sleep? Who would take care of it while all of us were away each day at school or work? Good questions, we all gravely agreed.

She also worried that this adoption seemed rather—what's the right word here?—casual. Apparently, "adopting" the animals in the zoo was simply a matter of putting a quite modest check in the mail. Adoption, in fact, meant nothing more than a fully revocable pledge to donate a few dollars to the zoo, which would be folded into the operating costs. Our daughter's distress reminded us that we had all of us, Jennifer as much or more than the rest, invested a great deal of time and anxiety and love to build the adoptive family we had.

We decided not to adopt any of the zoo's animals, but in the years since that memorable summer day, opportunities to "adopt" something or other have done nothing but multiply.

You can still adopt an animal: I have found more internet sites offering penguins for adoption than there are penguins in all of America's zoos. If penguins are not your animal of choice, you could adopt a lion or a tiger or a bear. If animals don't do it, you can adopt a classroom, or a tree, or a soldier (that one surprised me), or a section of highway, or a ship, or any one of several archaeological artifacts in the University of Pennsylvania Museum, or a Shakespearean actor at London's Globe Theatre.

I open with this small story to illustrate one of the themes I will be examining in this book: adoption is an exceptionally elusive term. The meaning of adoption, both literally and symbolically, has varied widely over time and place. Practices called adoption have ranged from the informal and often temporary care of a child (or adult) to the legal and permanent inclusion of a child into a new family, with several stops in between. *West's Encyclopedia of American Law* defines adoption as "the taking of a child into one's family, creating a parent to child relationship, and giving him or her all the rights and privileges of one's own child, including the right to inherit as if the child were the adopter's natural child." While this rhymes with our more or less common sense understanding, it doesn't begin to capture the variety and complexity of the practices we will review. Children have been adopted, legally and extra-legally, formally and informally, to constitute or re-constitute families, to provide homes when birth parents could not or would not do so, to serve as slaves, on the one hand, or to replace disinherited or deceased heirs on the other.

In this book, I have set out to provide a brief but reliable survey of the history of adoption, incorporating my reading and my personal experience as part of an adoptive family. In addition and more significantly, I want to reveal the complex nature of adoptive kinship, and its different meanings in diverse cultural contexts. In the course of the exposition, I hope that readers will come to understand that families really do come

DOI: 10.1057/9781137333919

in all shapes and flavors. As Kwame Anthony Appiah has put it, describing Ghanaian family structure, and in doing so summarizing a thesis I explore throughout the book: "There are, in short, different ways of organizing family life."[1]

Adoption's history, much of it largely forgotten, deserves recovery for several reasons. To begin with, the numbers of adoptive parents and children have grown dramatically since the Second World War, both in the United States and globally. In addition, according to a 1997 survey, "six in 10 Americans have had experience with adoption, meaning that they themselves, a family member or close friend was adopted, had adopted a child or placed a child for adoption."[2] And many other Americans have considered adoption.

Those millions of adults and children, who are re-shaping the meaning of family, have an obvious and personal stake in this subject. However, adoption's history and significance offer instruction for all of us, whether touched directly by adoption or not, about an increasingly important dimension of contemporary experience.

Beyond that, attitudes toward adoption can provide insight into larger cultural assumptions: not only about family and kinship, but also about race and ethnicity, about the law, about human nature itself. Many of the questions that adoption raises continue to be controversial, at once symptoms and causes of deep divides in values and perception. Because adoption's implications are multifarious, any inquiry into its social and cultural history will entail excursions into philosophy, sociology and anthropology, religion, law, research on animal behavior, personal experience, and the arts, especially literature.

And the occasional *New Yorker* cartoon caption: "Is that baby adopted, or artisanal?"

Finally, as I hope these chapters will demonstrate, the story of adoption is a veritable ripping yarn, filled with unexpected, exciting, sometimes downright implausible twists and turns, and a sensational cast of historical and fictional players. We will find Moses, and Julius Caesar, and Tarzan, along with Oedipus and memorable characters from the works of Shakespeare, Dickens, Philip Roth, Joyce Carol Oates, Chang-rae Lee, A. M. Homes, Eli Wiesel, Garrison Keillor, P. D. James, and Bill Cosby. We will encounter a Chinese emperor who adopted several hundred soldiers, apparently to invigorate their fighting spirits; an ancient Egyptian bureaucrat who adopted his wife as his daughter to secure her rights to inherit; a nineteenth-century American general who adopted the

DOI: 10.1057/9781137333919

children of Indians he had slaughtered; twentieth-century white Arizona townsmen who abducted white children from their Mexican adoptive parents; and non-human primates who exhibit undeniably adoptive behavior. Among many others.

I begin the first chapter with another family story.

Notes

1   Kwame Anthony Appiah, *Cosmopolitanism: Ethics in a World of Strangers* (New York: W. W. Norton & Company, 2006), p. 49.
2   "Benchmark Adoption Survey: Report on the Findings," Conducted for the Evan B. Donaldson Adoption Institute by Princeton Survey Research Associates (October, 1997).

DOI: 10.1057/9781137333919

1
Doing What Comes Naturally

Conn, Peter. *Adoption: A Brief Social and Cultural History*. New York: Palgrave Macmillan, 2013.
DOI: 10.1057/9781137333919.

▶

In 1976, on an otherwise pleasant weekend afternoon in March, my wife Terry and I confronted a serio-comic dilemma. We were filling in one of (what seemed like) several thousand forms required to legalize the adoption of our Korean daughter, Jennifer, in the Commonwealth of Pennsylvania.

Jennifer was our fourth child, and the first we had adopted. Jennifer had come to us, at a bit over two years old—her birth date is uncertain—malnourished and covered with sores, from an orphanage outside Seoul, a place with a fifty percent mortality rate. Which is to say, children either got out fairly quickly or they died. Korea's laws and customs conspired to make it almost certain that Jennifer would not find a home in her own country.

Given these high stakes, Terry and I were studiously patient with any and all red tape and inefficiency. Until Jennifer's adoption was final, she could, at least in theory, be taken from us and sent back. So we paid numberless fees and filled out countless forms. Knowing how urgent our task was, Terry and I plodded through the paperwork, meekly and honestly answering every question, however intrusive, until we came to this one:

"How many natural children do you have?"

We paused. We groaned. We laughed. We knew what the Commonwealth's bureaucrats meant. They thought they were asking: "how many non-adoptive children do you have?"

In fact, the bureaucrats had tripped over an obvious but venerable semantic mistake. Think about it. If the three children we already had, who had joined our family via the more traditional reproductive route, were "natural," then poor Jennifer was being consigned to a bin labeled "unnatural."

I used to tell this story as a small joke. It is not a joke. Many years ago, John Stuart Mill described the word "unnatural" as "one of the most vituperative epithets in the language," an assessment that remains true a century and a half later.[1]

We drafted a long, respectful letter, in which we thought we might enclose an edited version of the requisite form in which we would cross out "natural" and replace it with "non-adoptive."[2] Writing the letter made us feel better for an hour or two, but then we came to our senses, deposited our unsent letter in the nearest waste basket, and simply complied with the form's demand. We couldn't risk the delay

DOI: 10.1057/9781137333919

that would surely follow any argument with the commonwealth's functionaries.

"Three natural children," we testified through clenched teeth.

I use the story to introduce the subject of this first chapter: just what is "natural"?

There may not be a more vexed or vexatious word in the English language. "Nature," and its adjectival sibling, "natural," have an exceptionally complicated, contentious, and sometimes downright contradictory history. Raymond Williams, in his influential book *Keywords*, called it "perhaps the most complex word in the language." Williams identified three large, overlapping but distinct areas of meaning: the essential character of something, the inherent force that directs individuals and the world, and the material world itself.[3]

Whether intentionally or not, in emphasizing the elusiveness of "nature" Williams was following John Stuart Mill. In the posthumously published essay, "Nature," Mill observes that the word, in its various forms, is at once ubiquitous and opaque. Used indiscriminately to denote so many different entities and phenomena, nature has become a cause of confusion rather than clarity:

> Nature, natural, and the group of words derived from them, or allied to them in etymology, have at all times filled a great place in the thoughts and taken a strong hold on the feelings of mankind. That they should have done so is not surprising, when we consider what the words, in their primitive and most obvious signification, represent; but it is unfortunate that they [have become] one of the most copious sources of false taste, false philosophy, false morality, and even bad law.[4]

Today, most of us would associate the word "nature" with the third of Raymond Williams's definitions: the visible world, and specifically the parts of the world that have not been manufactured or altered by humans—sea and sky, plants and animals, clouds and mountains, rivers and forests.

Or, in the grander language of the *Oxford English Dictionary*, "nature" denotes (among many other things), "A state unaffected by human intervention; *spec.* (with reference to plants or animals) a wild condition that is not the result of cultivation, breeding, or rearing; (with reference to minerals or land) an uncultivated, unworked, or undeveloped state."

This is the nature of Wordsworth and Romantic poetry, the nature that "never did betray the heart that loved her," the nature of unspoiled

DOI: 10.1057/9781137333919

views and birdsong, the nature that offers a retreat from the noise and congestion of the modern city.

Mother Nature: nurturing, simple, warm, safe.

Something like pastoral is at work here, a genre that can be traced back to the Greeks and Romans. Poems of this type attach moral significance to the contrast between city and country: immorality and sophisticated forms of vice lurk in the city, while the country is the abode of innocence and simplicity. It is, after all, the place of the natural.

That combination of aesthetic and moral judgment has lingered to this day. Rural second homes afford affluent city-dwellers temporary escape from their hectic urban lives, and from the dangers that have always lurked in cities. Even politics resonates with the echoes of old pastoral hierarchies: "real Americans," we are often told, live in small towns, in the "heartland," anywhere other than the urbanized Left and Right Coasts.

Those small towns, which Americans have in fact been abandoning for over a century, retain the symbolic allure of "authenticity." Here is where a cluster of earlier and allegedly superior American values still repose, where neighborly and face-to-face transactions take place between people who know and trust one another. The myth has survived its repeated disproof. (Among other disproofs, crime is now a bigger problem in rural and suburban locales than in most American cities.)

That assumption of authenticity hovers over the idea of the "natural." It is the "way things are": to invoke nature is to claim the legitimacy of the presumed order of things. What is not natural—to reflect again on our scuffle with Pennsylvania's adoption bureaucrats—is more or less self-evidently artificial, something that has been made up, invented rather than simply "there." An essay on adoption in nineteenth-century Japan opens with the sentence, "Adoption is a long-standing system of fictional kinship." And a recent book on adoption in early modern France bears the title *Blood Ties and Fictive Ties*.[5]

And of course what is fictional is patently not natural. Meeting our adopted Korean daughter for the first time, well-meaning strangers would often ask whether we also had children "of our own." That phrase is one of the many ways in which ordinary language choices stigmatize adoptive kinship. Barely concealed under this question is the assertion, if not "our own," then someone else's, and not ours at all.

This is not a new attitude. Back in 1929, social work educator Jessie Taft had this to say on the subject: "No one who is not wilfully deluded

DOI: 10.1057/9781137333919

would maintain that the experiences of adoption can take the place of the actual bearing and rearing of an own child."⁶

This sad comment is made even more self-lacerating by the fact that Jessie Taft was the mother of two children, both of them adopted.

What is fictional is also not real. In an essay called "Kith and Kin," Julian Pitt-Rivers observes that the people of several regions, including southern Spain, Mexico, and Peru, "commonly distinguish between 'real' kinship and adopted kin; and the distinction is significant, since only the 'real' kin are fully part of the kinship system."⁷

Full disclosure. Our daughter Jennifer apparently once agreed that adoption does not bring "real" kinship. On a memorable afternoon in 1978, three years after her arrival, and in the midst of an argument about something or other now long forgotten by both of us, she paused, lifted her five-year-old self to her full height, pierced me with a steely gaze, and announced in a low, steady voice: "You are not my real father. I am going back to Korea to find my real father."

Now, I had been prepared for this moment. During the long adoption process, our ever-cheerful social worker had warned me that such statements are not uncommon, that I should not be alarmed, that Jennifer would almost certainly not resort to this particular tactic more than a couple of times, that she wouldn't really mean it—in short, keep it in perspective, and all would soon be well.

Despite all that sensible advice, my immediate reaction to Jennifer's declaration was, of course, to burst into tears. My blubbering, apparently, was more than she had bargained for. She instantly transformed herself from adversary into nurse and did what she could to console me. Nonetheless, her accusation proved that she instinctively understood the power of the word "real."⁸

Years ago, in a provocative book called *American Kinship: A Cultural Account*, David Schneider investigated what he called the "two orders" of kinship that Americans used to distinguish human relationships: the order of nature and the order of law. The "order of nature" includes persons who share the same substance, specifically the same blood; these are relationships constructed in biogenetic terms, and derived from sexual intercourse. According to Schneider, these connections are perceived by Americans to be objective, permanent, and unalterable. The "order of law," by contrast, includes persons related by choices such as marriage and adoption. Such relationships, Schneider argues, are not understood by Americans to have the "strength" of biogenetic ties.⁹

DOI: 10.1057/9781137333919

Because it is seen to lie outside the order of nature, adoption's assumed eccentricity—indeed its presumptive deviance—is sometimes revealed by its absence from explorations of the family.[10] In *The History of the Family*, for example, James Casey surveys one thousand years of family life, in Europe and around the world. Casey's fairly recent and quite impressive book is based, as R. I. Moore says in his editor's preface, on the conviction that the ways in which families are constructed are "infinitely variable." Well, not quite. While Casey finds room for everything from aborigines to concubinage to wet-nursing, adoption is not mentioned.[11]

A 400-page textbook called *The American Family: Past, Present, and Future*, includes just a single, two-page discussion of adoption, and only in connection with one-parent adoption. Similarly, in another 400-page volume called *American Families: A Research Guide and Historical Handbook*, the sole mention of adoption deals with the children of single, unwed mothers.

The Atlas of European Values includes a twenty-plus-page section on "Family," replete with charts, graphs, and texts, but with no mention of adoption. A textbook on "changing perspectives" in American family law excludes adoption altogether.[12] A recent collection of twenty essays, gathered in a volume called *American Families Past and Present*, examines subjects including fertility, illegitimacy, grandparents, child care, and wedding dresses; adoption is barely mentioned. Even an essay specifically addressed to "Historical Perspectives on Family Diversity" manages to exclude adoption from its analysis.[13]

I could multiply examples, but will add only one more. A book called *American Family History: A Historical Bibliography* (1984) contains 1,167 entries, of which a total of one deals with adoption.

When it isn't invisible, adoption can even be dangerous, as this passage from Philip Roth's *The Anatomy Lesson* vividly suggests. Nathan Zuckerman's college friend Bobby Freytag, a successful anesthesiologist in Chicago, was sterilized in adolescence and has adopted a child, Gregory. Gregory turns out to be a monster of ingratitude, insensitivity, and selfishness. Bobby's father finds all the explanation he needs in the fact of adoption itself:

> "[A] son who tells his father to eat shit! Would Bobby have produced, on his own, a boy so full of contempt? He would have had a child who has *feelings*, feelings like *we* have feelings. A child who worked and who studied and who stayed home, and who wanted to excel like his father . . . . Because who is he? Do we even know where he comes from? She [Bobby's then-wife] wanted a

DOI: 10.1057/9781137333919

baby, little orphan baby, and what in his roots that we don't know makes him behave this way to Bobby? I have a brilliant son. And all that brilliance locked in his genes! Everything we gave him, trapped like that in Bobby's genes, while everything we are *not*, everything we are *against*—How can all this end with Gregory?"¹⁴

Here is where the idea of nature as the proper order of things intersects the concept of nature as inherently moral. What nature—and, for centuries, nature's God—has decreed is what is right. And what nature has decreed was and remains reproductive kinship. Recall that the English word "nature" derives ultimately from the Latin "to be born." The etymology reinforces the inevitability and irreversibility of the term. To quote John Stuart Mill again, "*Naturam sequi* [to follow nature] was the fundamental principle of morals in many of the most admired schools of philosophy."¹⁵ Small wonder that several of the world's major religions have discouraged and in some cases prohibited adoption, a subject to which I will return.

This view of nature as legitimacy's self-evident source has generated centuries of philosophical and theological elaboration. I attended a Dominican college in which I spent several semesters in the obligatory study of what was called "the natural law." Our source books included several works of Aristotle, including the *Nichomachean Ethics*, the *Politics*, and the *Rhetoric* (in English translation) and *The Summa Theologica* of Thomas Aquinas (in Latin).

By the term "natural law," the Dominicans did not mean "laws of nature," in the modern, scientific sense: i.e., if I drop a stone it will invariably fall down instead of up (barring a once-in-several-trillion-trillion-occurrences quantum anomaly); if I put heat under a pot of water it will inevitably experience a phase change and commence to boil at 100 degrees Celsius; and so on.

The laws of nature tell us how the physical world actually works. On the contrary, according to my Dominican teachers, natural law tells us how the moral world *should* work. In a tradition reaching back to Aristotle and beyond, and forward to the twenty-first century, dozens of major Western philosophers have affirmed one version or another of natural law. While each version differs in larger or smaller detail, just about all of these theories propose that the moral standards governing human behavior are derived—how is generally left unexplained—directly from the inborn nature of human beings.

Thus the concept of "human nature," a phrase that has been the focus of philosophical debate for centuries. In a recent survey of the concept,

DOI: 10.1057/9781137333919

Peter Lopson examines eleven major theories of human nature, commencing with Aristotle, and proceeding more or less chronologically through the arguments of John Locke, Immanuel Kant, and Jean Jacques Rousseau to the hypotheses of Charles Darwin and Sigmund Freud, among others.[16]

What is natural self-evidently comprises the proper order of things, whether in personal behavior or politics—and not just temporarily but permanently. This account of nature is perfectly compatible with religious belief, but can also supersede belief. In Guy Robinson's version of Enlightenment thought, "Nature was meant to stand over and above and outside of the happenings of this world in the way God had."[17] Since nature lies behind and above the particular circumstances of life, its demands are unchanging: what was true and right in the past remains true and right today. In short, the customary power of nature and the natural have conspired against non-reproductive kinship, and continue to do so, less explicitly to be sure but no less influentially than in the past.[18]

Adoption is not the only human institution that calls into question nature's authority as a moral guide. As many scholars have pointed out, "nature" has historically served as a tool of mystification and often of oppression. Across centuries of human history, and to give just a partial list, the following have been considered natural: the existence of God, monarchy and other systems of hierarchical governance, primogeniture, slavery, the subordination of girls and women, and heterosexuality. Women and slaves, who between them have made up the majority of the human race throughout its history, have also and almost universally been consigned to positions of (allegedly) natural inferiority.

These observations merit our attention because, as we will see, adoption is not only another instance of the traditionally unnatural, but has itself been a transaction profoundly affected by gender and race.

The natural inferiority of women has been a centerpiece of Western philosophy and culture from the Greeks forward. Plato argued that the lesser humanity of women could be understood as a form of degeneration from maleness. "According to our likely account, all male-born humans who lived lives of cowardice or injustice were reborn in the second generation as women."[19] How that "second generation" was generated, by the way, Plato does not say.

For Aristotle, a woman was "an inferior man," and "defective by nature." The innate superiority of men is proved by their role in reproduction,

DOI: 10.1057/9781137333919

since semen is the active agent in conception. Women merely provide the receptacle—the "flower pot," in Caroline Whitbeck's wry phrase—for generation.[20] For Aristotle, the subordination of women to men resembles the relationship between men and tame animals.

Mythology buttressed philosophy. To be sure, the Greco–Roman pantheon is crowded with powerful female deities, but all of them remain subordinate to ultimate male authority, and quite a few of them are troublesome busybodies—the interfering crone next door on a cosmic scale. Medusa, with her hair full of snakes and her talent for turning men into stone, embodies the dangers of female power and sexuality. And recall that mythology's first mortal woman, Pandora, is notorious for releasing all of humanity's troubles. In Judeao–Christian mythology, it is usually Eve who gets more blame for the Fall than Adam.

Over the two millennia that followed the Greeks, a long list of philosophers and social theorists—many of whom agreed about nothing else—concurred in assuming the natural inferiority of women. There is no need to itemize this depressing but familiar catalogue of discrimination at length: selected low points will serve.

Medieval European literature is filled with the "ritual denunciation of women," to use R. Howard Bloch's phrase: "It dominates ecclesiastical writing, letters, sermons, theological tracts, discussions and compilations of canon law; scientific works, as part and parcel of biological, gynaecological, and medical knowledge; and philosophy."[21] Much of this richly noisome literature was of course grounded in appeals to nature and the natural.

John Milton shared the commonplace view of women as subservient and subordinate, and created in Eve a character who personified physical weakness, limited intelligence, and moral fragility. Above all, Eve is properly submissive:

> For contemplation he and valour formed,
>
> For softness she and sweet attractive grace;
>
> He for God only, she for God in him.[22]

A generation later, John Locke declared that the final decision in family life "falls to the man's share as the abler and stronger."[23] David Hume, in his essay "On the Immortality of the Soul" (1783), took female inferiority to be more or less self-evident: "... the inferiority of women's capacity is easily accounted for. Their domestic life requires no higher faculties

DOI: 10.1057/9781137333919

either of mind or body."[24] In other words, cleaning and cooking don't require the elevated "faculties" of a philosopher.

Jean Jacques Rousseau also insisted on the natural inferiority of women. In *Émile*, Rousseau insisted that the "very law of nature," which denies men certitude about the paternity of their children, logically leads to the subordination of women.

What is it with these men and their nightmares over blood kinship? They might take a cue from the sardonic advice offered by the Captain in August Strindberg's *The Father*:

> Good Lord, that is my child! Mine? We can never know. Do you know what we would have to do to make sure? First, one should marry to get the respect of society, then be divorced soon after and become lovers, and finally adopt the children. Then one would at least be sure that they were one's adopted children.[25]

But back to Rousseau. After quoting his declaration that the uncertainty of parentage demands the subordination of women, philosopher Susan Moller Okin comments, "Thus nature necessitates women's subjection to men, and the imperfections of men's nature necessitate the reinforcement of women's natural propensity for enduring injustice."

After savoring that paradox, Okin formulates the question with which I am concerned in this chapter: "But what on earth, we must ask, is 'nature'?"[26]

Okin contends that families have been excluded from almost all theories of justice because they were assumed to be "natural" institutions, and thus outside the reach of such speculation. The result, of course, has been to affirm by neglect that traditional patriarchal values define the domestic space in which women and children live. Making a similar point, Sally Haslanger has observed that insofar as "the natural nuclear family schema...underwrites traditional gender roles and heternormative models of the family, I take it to be morally problematic."[27]

Once again, John Stuart Mill offers the best comment: "Was there ever any domination which did not appear natural to those who possessed it?"[28]

The allegedly natural domination of men over women has been repeated in the domination of masters over slaves. From Chinese dynasties in the first millennium BCE, through the Mediterranean world of Greece, Rome, and medieval Europe, across much of the Near East, large sections of Africa, and of course North and South America, slavery in one form or another was a persistent and prominent feature of social organization. In his ambitious and provocative survey, *Slavery and Social Death*, Orlando Patterson gathered information from sixty-six slaveholding societies; in an appendix, he also listed 200 large-scale slave systems, including the slavery practiced by Saharan Tuaregs in the 1960s. Mauritania, the last country in the world to abolish slavery, did so as recently as 1981, and only in 2007 made the ownership of another person a criminal offense.

Made familiar through near-universal custom, slavery was vigorously defended as natural by its practitioners.[29] Such defenses can be traced back to classical Greece and Rome, and forward into the nineteenth century.

The world's major religions, which have conspired for centuries in the subordination of women, performed the same role in affirming the rectitude of slavery. As recently as 1866, just a year after the end of the Civil War, in which 600,000 Americans had died in a bloody struggle that finally extinguished the crime of chattel slavery in the United States, Pope Pius IX had this to say about the practice:

> Slavery itself, considered as such in its essential nature, is not at all contrary to the natural and divine law, and there can be several just titles of slavery and these are referred to by approved theologians and commentators of the sacred canons.... It is not contrary to the natural and divine law for a slave to be sold, bought, exchanged or given.[30]

Slavery is "not contrary to the natural and divine law": this from the man who, four years later, declared himself infallible.

By now, the consternation that Terry and I felt when our baby daughter was being indirectly but decisively labeled "not natural" should be clear. I do not claim that Pennsylvania's rule makers intended the stigma they implied. I do claim that the age-old association of "nature" and non-adoptive parenthood has thickened the atmosphere of disapproval surrounding adoption.

Let me now take the discussion in a different direction. Precisely because "nature" has been so consistently used as a mechanism of subordination and even oppression, a great deal of energy has gone into a revisionist project. In this undertaking, social scientists and philosophers have worked to identify the hidden force of custom and familiarity in shaping beliefs and behaviors that have been called natural.

DOI: 10.1057/9781137333919

I return to John Stuart Mill, and his essay "Nature." After reviewing the traditional power of the term as a marker of legitimacy, Mill argues that nature has no connection to such concepts as justice or the good: "Conformity to nature has no connection whatever with right and wrong." On the contrary, Nature is a continual source of suffering and evil.

> Killing, the most criminal act recognised by human laws, Nature does once to every being that lives; and, in a large proportion of cases, after protracted tortures such as only the greatest monsters whom we read of ever purposely inflicted on their living fellow creatures.

With rhetorical exuberance, Mill itemizes Nature's crimes against humanity:

> Nature impales men, breaks them as if on the wheel, casts them to be devoured by wild beasts, burns them to death, crushes them with stones like the first Christian martyr, starves them with hunger, freezes them with cold, poisons them by the quick or slow venom of her exhalations, and has hundreds of other hideous deaths in reserve .... [31]

Mill's bumptious vocabulary represents a calculated effort to shock his readers out of whatever sentimental and reverent opinions they might entertain. Although he was an admirer of Wordsworth's poetry, Mill nonetheless insisted on a sharp distinction between the (ultimately trivial) comforts that might be found in a charming landscape and the (ultimately profound) devastation that natural forces inflict on all men and women. His tone is deliberately melodramatic, but his comments merely confirm what all of us know.

As he goes on to point out, if we really believed in Nature's benevolence, "then everything done by mankind which tends to chain up these natural agencies or to restrict their mischievous operations from draining a pestilential marsh down to curing the toothache, or putting up an umbrella, ought to be accounted impious; which assuredly nobody does account them."

A few pages ago, I noted that the antonyms of "natural" included "artificial," a term that has been used to demean adoptive relationships. Mill's answer turns the distinction on its head: "If the artificial is not better than the natural, to what end are all the arts of life? To dig, to plough, to build, to wear clothes, are direct infringements of the injunction to follow nature."

Behind Mill's re-definition of "nature," as a set of antagonistic forces better opposed than revered, stands a long counter-history of the term.

DOI: 10.1057/9781137333919

In a passage I quoted earlier, Raymond Williams proposed that "nature" is perhaps the most complex word in the English language; part of the reason lies in its downright self-contradictory implications.

In this less well-known narrative, nature is a place of disorder, outside the reach of law and teetering on the edge of anarchy. This is the "state of nature" that Thomas Hobbes explored, the realm of all against all, a theater of bloody competition for domination. According to Hobbes, human beings need to organize themselves and submit to authority in order to escape their natural inclinations. Life in these primitive circumstances, Hobbes argued, is "solitary, poor, nasty, brutish, and short." Until they create civil government, men and women are in that condition "which is called war; and such a war as is of every man against every man."[32]

Hobbes did not invent this dystopian view of nature. Here is the speech through which Edmund introduces himself in *King Lear*:

> Thou, Nature, art my goddess; to thy law
> My services are bound. Wherefore should I
> Stand in the plague of custom, and permit
> The curiosity of nations to deprive me,
> For that I am some twelve or fourteen moon-shines
> Lag of a brother? Why bastard? wherefore base?
> ......
> Who, in the lusty stealth of nature, take
> More composition and fierce quality
> Than doth, within a dull, stale, tired bed,
> Go to the creating a whole tribe of fops,
> Got 'tween asleep and wake? Well, then,
> Legitimate Edgar, I must have your land:
> Our father's love is to the bastard Edmund
> As to the legitimate: fine word,—legitimate!
> Well, my legitimate, if this letter speed,
> And my invention thrive, Edmund the base
> Shall top the legitimate. I grow; I prosper:
> Now, gods, stand up for bastards![33]

Edmund, one of Shakespeare's supreme villains, invokes Nature as his goddess. Here is a different "nature" altogether: not the unspoiled landscape and the habitation of consoling rustic deities, nor the unerring source of proper personal and political judgment, but the realm of the barbarous and the unlawful.

DOI: 10.1057/9781137333919

In this case, and despite what I wanted to tell the adoption bureaucrats in Pennsylvania, "natural" here does not imply "unnatural" as its antonym. On the contrary, in the dark world of *King Lear*, "natural" stands opposed to "legitimate," to lawful, to the whole system of justice and order that makes civilized society possible. As many of the play's readers have pointed out, the language of *King Lear* creates a universe of natural cruelty. The great Shakespearean scholar A. C. Bradley famously offered what he called a partial list of the metaphors that are summoned to describe the play's characters and the world they inhabit:

> The dog, the horse, the cow, the sheep, the hog, the lion, the bear, the wolf, the fox, the monkey, the pole-cat, the civet-cat, the pelican, the owl, the crow, the chough, the wren, the fly, the butterfly, the rat, the mouse, the frog, the tadpole, the wall-newt, the water-newt, the worm....[34]

When he names Nature as his "goddess," Edmund would have been disclosing not only his moral quality but also the circumstances of his birth. Shakespeare's Elizabethan audience commonly used the term "natural" to describe an illegitimate child. This is why he demands that the gods (and goddesses) "stand up for bastards."[35]

Mother Nature, indeed.

So, when we were asked how many natural children we had, we might have answered, "None. All were born after our marriage."

Our excursion through the tangled history of "nature" has led us to the recognition that a meditation on adoption can help dismantle supposedly common sense notions of family creation. There is no innate hierarchy among families. Susan Okin has argued that human nature, if the term means anything at all, is pliable and changeable: "it is not something which is fixed and will continue to be fixed for all time, but is rather an achievement, a result of thousands of years of history."[36]

As early as the 1930s, Ruth Benedict argued that we make a profound mistake when we equate "our local normalities with the inevitable necessities of existence...."[37] What we take to be natural, whether in kinship formation or human hierarchy, is the result of generations of human negotiation.

David Schneider entered a similar rebuttal to the automatic definition of birth parentage as "natural" and therefore superior:

> So much of kinship and family in American culture is defined as being nature itself, required by nature, or directly determined by nature that it is quite difficult, often impossible, in fact, for Americans to see this as a set

DOI: 10.1057/9781137333919

of cultural constructs and not the biological facts themselves. They see the facts of flesh and blood as the pertinent facts, the facts which contain the actual identity of parent and child, which contain the force which compels the deep feeling and love between the two, and which makes them "only natural."[38]

Needless to say, I admire Schneider's vigorous dissent from a specimen of conventional wisdom disguised as truth. I am, however, tempted to go further than merely re-arranging the hierarchy of human identity, and to endorse Guy Robinson's more radical critique: "the notion of 'human nature' is a blank with no explanatory force, despite the great use that is made of it." For Robinson, both "nature" and "human nature" are "empty notions that don't advance things any, and the determinism they threaten is no more than a spook, the ghost of our own misunderstandings."[39]

In those philosophy courses I took years ago at Providence College, we were taught to distinguish between the "essence" of a thing and its "accidents." As it turned out, the accidents comprised everything that could actually be known about any entity, whether the entity was human, animal, vegetable, or inanimate matter. Accidents included size, shape, color, weight, and all the other variables that can be measured. Essence referred, on the other hand, to the invisible, unmeasurable innermost quality that actually defined the entity. And essence, I eventually concluded, was mere mumbo-jumbo, a figure of speech, an empty word. The "essence" of horse was... horseness. The essence of tree was treeness. And so on. And on.

"Nature," despite its respectable place in centuries of philosophical discussion, seems to me hardly more robust than scholastic essence. The very complexity of the term and its multiform and often contradictory significations defeat coherent definition. Where is it located? What are its undeniable signs? What, to put it bluntly, is the proof of its existence beyond its traditional, familiar, and customary invocations?

I will not, of course, deny that human beings are embedded in the natural world, using the word "natural" here simply to denote the third and least mystical of Raymond Williams's definitions: the palpable, biological stuff of planet Earth. I also acknowledge that many of our actions are automatic. We seem to be hard-wired for certain activities— among them eating, copulating, ducking away from a high, inside fastball. However, that limited repertoire of instinctive behaviors does not and should not lead to overarching, determinist generalizations about "human nature."

DOI: 10.1057/9781137333919

I will return to these questions in subsequent chapters, in particular when I review the controversies surrounding interracial and intercountry adoption. I will suggest that the recurrent demand for "matching," whether along lines of ethnicity or religion or country of birth—or, believe it or not, skin shade, eye color, even hair tone—resurrects a discredited appeal to both essence and nature.

Adoption has needed a Franz Boas, the great German–American anthropologist who in the early twentieth century moved the study of culture away from invidious comparisons between the primitive and the civilized—the lower and higher, in other words—and toward more humane explorations of cultural differences on their own terms. In that spirit, I will argue that adoptive families should be understood not as second-best deviations from some order of nature but instead as positive metaphors, emblems of an increasingly interconnected, global, hybridized, and mobile humanity.

Before embarking on those topics, let me review in the next two chapters the histories of adoption, globally and in America.

Notes

1   John Stuart Mill, "Nature," in Louis J. Matz, ed., *Three Essays on Religion* (Rutgers, NJ: Broadview Editions, 2009), p. 70. Ironically, today's journalists tend to reserve the adjective "unnatural" for crimes against children.

2   Adoptive parents have always struggled to find a suitable term for their non-adoptive children that avoids the pitfalls of "natural." Some of the alternatives—e.g., "biological children" or "birth children"—bring problems of their own, since all children, whether adopted or not, are biological and were born. I like "non-adoptive," both because it is distinctively accurate and because in a sneaky way it suggests that adoption might be the norm.

3   Raymond Williams, *Keywords: A Vocabulary of Culture and Society*, revised edn (New York: Oxford University Press, 1983), p. 219.

4   John Stuart Mill, "Nature," p. 65.

5   Satomi Kurosu and Emiko Ochiai, "Adoption as an Heirship Strategy under Demographic Constraints: A Case from Nineteenth-Century Japan," *Journal of Family History*, vol. 20, no. 3 (1995), pp. 261–288. Kristin Elizabeth Gager, *Blood Ties and Fictive Ties: Adoption and Family Life in Early Modern France* (Princeton, 1996).

6   Jessie Taft, "Concerning Adopted Children," *Child Study*, vol. 6 (1929), p. 87; cited in Ellen Herman, "Can Kinship Be Designed and Still Be Normal?

DOI: 10.1057/9781137333919

The Curious Case of Child Adoption," in Waltraud Ernst, ed., *Histories of the Normal and the Abnormal: Social and Cultural Histories of Norms and Normativity* (London: Routledge, 2006), p. 205. "Own" is another complex word, combining meanings of "to oneself" and "having the title to," as in property.

7   Julian Pitt-Rivers, "The Kith and the Kin," in Jack Goody, ed., *The Character of Kinship* (London: Cambridge University Press, 1973), p. 94. This volume contains fourteen essays, and, despite the comprehensive expectations that the book's title raises, Pitt-Rivers's brief account of "real" vs. adopted in some cultures is the only engagement with adoption.

8   According to Marshall Schecter, adopted children have trouble coping with two sets of parents, adoptive vs. what he calls "real," since the perception interferes with their "Oedipal development." We will have occasion later in this chapter to see more evidence of the baleful influence of Freudian claptrap on real, as opposed to "real," lives. Marshall Schecter, "Observations on Adopted Children," *A.M.A. Archives of General Psychiatry*, vol. 3, no. 1 (1960), pp. 21–32.

9   David Schneider, *American Kinship: A Cultural Account*, 2nd edn (Chicago: University of Chicago Press, 1980), pp. 24ff.

10 Adoption has generated a long shelf of books, but most of them are technical guides, social work manuals, psychological studies, and legal surveys that treat adoption as a separated—I am tempted to say segregated— phenomenon. Adoption has mainly been missing from broader histories of the family.

11 James Casey, *The History of the Family* (Oxford: Basil Blackwell, 1989). Casey usefully argues that "the discovery of the family as a problem begins with the economic and political upheavals of the nineteenth century. The collapse of the old hierarchy induced a range of talented thinkers in Western Europe to elaborate some ideas of how societies were held together in the first place: if not by the force of the state, then by what?" (p. 14) Casey proposes that the family is a moral system, not just an institution, a suggestion that makes his omission of adoption all the more notable.

12 Patricia McGee Crotty, *Family Law in the United States: Changing Perspectives* (New York: Peter Lang, 1999).

13 Loek Halman, Ruud Luijkx, and Marga van Zundert, eds, *Atlas of European Values* (Leiden: Tilbert University, 2005), pp. 24–42. Susan M. Ross, ed., *American Families Past and Present: Social Perspectives on Transformations* (New Brunswick, NJ: Rutgers University Press, 2006).

14 Philip Roth, *The Anatomy Lesson* (New York: Farrar, Straus and Giroux, 1983), p. 261.

15 John Stuart Mill, "Nature," p. 68.

16 Peter Lopson, *Theories of Human Nature*, 3rd edn (Peterborough, Canada: Broadview Guides to Philosophy, 2006).

DOI: 10.1057/9781137333919

17   Guy Robinson, *Philosophy and Mystification: A Reflection on Nonsense and Clarity* (London: Routledge, 1998), p. 231.

18   Introducing a collection of essays on the concepts of "normal" and "abnormal," Waltraud Ernst confuses matters with the sweeping claim that "[w]here we would now use the term 'normal,' pre-modern definitions referred to the 'natural.'" This is obviously wrong, since the term "natural" is still ubiquitous. Waltraud Ernst, ed., *Histories of the Normal and the Abnormal: Social and Cultural Histories or Norms and Normativity* (London: Routledge, 2006), i.

19   Plato, *Timaeus*, Donald J. Zeyl, trans. (Hackett Publishing, 2000), pp. 86–87.

20   Caroline Whitbeck, "Theories of Sex Difference," in Carol C. Gould and Marx W. Wartofsky, eds, *Women and Philosophy: Toward a Theory of Liberation* (New York: G. B. Putnam's Sons, 1976), p. 55.

21   R. Howard Bloch, "Medieval Misogyny," *Representations* (Autumn, 1987), p. 1.

22   John Milton, *Paradise Lost*, Book. IV, 295–299.

23   John Locke, *Second Treatise of Government*, J. W. Gough, ed. (Oxford: Basil Blackwell, 1948), p. 41.

24   David Hume, *On the Immortality of the Soul*, §II, 1783 (originally written in 1755).

25   August Strindberg, *The Father*, Act 3; *Plays: The Father; Countess Julie; The Outlaw; The Stranger*, Edith and Warner Oland, trans.; http://www.gutenberg. org/files/8499/8499-h/8499-h.htm#2H_4_0006 *[EBook #8499]*

26   Susan Moller Okin, *Justice, Gender, and the Family* (New York: Basic Books, 1989), pp. 33, 37.

27   Sally Haslanger, "Family, Ancestry and Self: What Is the Moral Significance of Biological Ties?" *Adoption and Culture*, vol. 2 (2009), p. 114. Haslanger concludes her essay with this demand: "... rather than enshrining a schema that most families fail to exemplify and which is used to stigmatize and alienate families that are (yes!) as good as their biological counterparts, we should instead make every effort to disrupt the hegemony of the schema" (p. 115).

28   John Stuart Mill, *The Subjection of Women*, Susan M. Okin, ed. (Indianapolis: Hackett Publishing Company, 1988), p. 12.

29   The defense of slavery's natural legitimacy often coincided with a bad conscience. Romans, for example, referred to slave trading as "*mercatura sordida*," a "dirty business." See Brent D. Shaw, "Introduction: A Wolf By the Ears," in his edition of M. I. Finley, *Ancient Slavery and Modern Ideology* (Princeton, NJ: Markus Wiener Publishers, 1980), p. 12.

30   Pius IX (*Instruction* 20 June 1866), cited in J. F. Maxwell, "The Development of Catholic Doctrine Concerning Slavery," *World Jurist*, 11 (1969–1970), pp. 306–307.

31   John Stuart Mill, "Nature," p. 81.

DOI: 10.1057/9781137333919

32 Thomas Hobbes, *Leviathan*, chapter XIII; http://www.gutenberg.org/files/3207/3207-h/3207-h.htm

33 William Shakespeare, *King Lear*, I, ii, pp. 1–24.

34 A. C. Bradley, *Shakespearean Tragedy: Lectures on Hamlet, Othello, King Lear, Macbeth*, 2nd edn (London: Macmillan, 1922 [1905]), p. 266.

35 The *Oxford English Dictionary* traces this use of "natural" back to the late fourteenth century.

36 Susan Moller Okin, *Justice, Gender, and the Family*, p. 298.

37 Ruth Benedict, *Patterns of Culture* (Boston: Houghton Mifflin Company, 1934), p. 374.

38 David Schneider, *American Kinship*, p. 116. In the opinion of anthropologist Anthony Good, "kinship is not a clearly delimited 'thing' but an amorphous polythetic concept." Anthony Good, "Kinship," in *Encyclopedia of Social and Cultural Anthropology* (New York: Routledge, 1996), p. 311. (I had to look up "polythetic," which means "having some but not all properties in common.")

39 Guy Robinson, *Philosophy and Mystification*, pp. 225, 274.

DOI: 10.1057/9781137333919

2

Adoption's Long and Often Surprising History

Conn, Peter. *Adoption: A Brief Social and Cultural History*. New York: Palgrave Macmillan, 2013.
DOI: 10.1057/9781137333919.

▶

DOI: 10.1057/9781137333919

The first surprise, at least to me, is that adoption occurs quite regularly among non-human primates, other animals, and even birds. To put it in the terms of Chapter 1, even in the animal kingdom, the meaning of "natural" is more elusive than we might expect.

Thirty years ago, Marianne Riedman summarized research to that date and concluded that alloparental care (i.e., surrogate parenting) and adoption of non-biogenetic young had been reported in over 120 mammalian and 150 avian species.[1] Those numbers have grown in the three decades since Riedman's article appeared, as observers have discovered instances of adoption, alloparenting, and fostering across additional species in all parts of the world. In a quite recent study, C. Daniel Batson concludes that adoption is in fact quite common throughout the animal kingdom, and is found "in a range of primate species, including humans, as well as in elephants, canids (wolves, dogs), rodents, a number of bird species, and, of course, the social insects."[2]

This is fascinating stuff. Let me share just a few examples from the hundreds of cases published in the research literature. In 1982, William J. Hamilton and his colleagues reported on adoption among baboons in Botswana. Pre-reproductive males and females, aged four and five years, adopted nine orphaned infants. While the scientists speculated that most of the adoptions involved close kin, two unrelated orphans introduced by the researchers were "immediately adopted" by five-year old males. In that same year, C. M. Berman observed the infant career of a rhesus monkey, orphaned at eleven weeks and cared for initially by four males and then by a sister who did not have other offspring. One conclusion: the animal seemed to suffer no long-term ill effects from his adoptive experience.[3]

More recently, after observing that "allomothering and adoption are well documented across primate species," Emily Wroblewski reported on a "unique incident" where an infant was adopted by its grandmother without the death of its mother. In another new finding, Romina Pave and her colleagues reported the first case of adoption in a wild group of black and gold howler monkeys. An orphaned infant was adopted by the mother's daughter and raised along with the daughter's offspring. Both infants seemed to receive equal treatment.[4]

Once they realized the frequency of surrogate parenting across the animal kingdom, the question that many primatologists have asked is no longer whether, but why? How does apparently altruistic behavior align with evolutionary theories of competition for reproductive advantage?

DOI: 10.1057/9781137333919

Given the counter-intuitive implications, it is not surprising that several theories have proposed that adoption among animals is not in fact altruistic, or that it represents only "reciprocal altruism"—you scratch my back and I'll scratch yours. Other contrarian hypotheses include the possibility of reproductive "mistakes" (a mother simply identifying an infant she did not bear), or the notion that adoption may provide "practice" for the females of some species who produce few offspring.

The emerging consensus, however, is that animals do display behaviors that appear to make robust claims on the concept of altruism. In a quite recent study, Christophe Boesch and colleagues reported on "potentially altruistic" behaviors among chimpanzees that included food sharing, regular use of coalitions, cooperative hunting and border patrolling. Most significantly, the researchers observed eighteen cases of adoption, including the adoption of young orphans by group members in forest chimpanzees in the Taï National Park, Côte d'Ivoire. Some adoptions of orphans by unrelated adult males lasted for years. This, Boesch and his co-workers accurately note, is "a highly costly behavior."[5]

Maybe adoption is "doing what comes naturally," after all.

To put it another way, and without resorting to sociobiological determinism, these examples of non-human adoption support the hypothesis that adoption, in all sorts of variations, may have at least some of its sources in our animal inheritance.[6]

In any case, it is reasonable to speculate that adoption has been practiced from the earliest societies of modern humans. Prehistoric life was short and frequently ended abruptly. When parents died, their orphaned children faced a perilous future, which ended in many cases in death by starvation or predation or human violence. But some of these children survived, and some form of adoption was surely one instrument of their survival. Whether on a large or small scale, and whether out of compassion, the desire for an heir, or the opportunity to acquire a servant, the circulation of abandoned children must have been a feature of those early communities.

Mesopotamia

My hypothesis is ultimately unprovable, since the first several hundred thousand years of modern human experience have left no written trace.

DOI: 10.1057/9781137333919

slightly paradoxical situation we will look at later, in which adoption was simultaneously discouraged by medieval Christian authorities but invoked as a figure of speech to indicate God's spiritual paternity.

Greece

The tale of the life and death of Oedipus has come down to us in several variations, most famously in Sophocles's drama of about 429 BCE. One of Western culture's founding stories, it has sometimes been read as a warning against adoption. I want to summarize the rudiments of the plot briefly and then offer a different interpretation.

Oedipus was the son of Laius, the king of Thebes, and his wife, Jocasta. Terrified by a prophecy that his son would murder him, Laius contrived to have the infant Oedipus killed. After the baby's ankles were cruelly bound together to prevent him from crawling, he was turned over to a servant to be exposed and left to die from starvation or killed by predators. Infanticide was a common practice in the ancient world, though usually for reasons less exotic than Laius's.

However, as almost every version of the story continues, Oedipus was spared death by a nameless servant who pitied him and passed him along to a shepherd. Eventually, Oedipus was taken to Corinth, and deposited in the house of King Polybus and his wife, Merope. Being childless, the royal couple adopted the baby and named him (rather unromantically: "Oedipus" derives from the Greek for swelling, to recall the damage to the boy's ankles from the tight ropes).

A story that begins with a miracle of deliverance ends in bloody tragedy. Informed that he has been adopted, Oedipus seeks the truth of his birth from the Oracle at Delphi—the same prophet from whom Laius had learned of the danger he faced from his son. Although she refuses to answer the question of parentage, the Oracle gives Oedipus the shattering revelation that he is destined to murder his father and marry his mother. Desperate to avoid this fate, Oedipus leaves Corinth and travels to Thebes. On the journey, at a crossing of three roads, Oedipus meets and kills a stranger in a fight over precedence. The stranger, of course, is Laius.

From here, the tale marches toward its fated end. His successful encounter with the Sphinx frees Thebes from the Sphinx's murderous rule. As a reward, Oedipus is made king, marries Jocasta, and has

DOI: 10.1057/9781137333919

four children with her. Years later, when a plague descends on Thebes, Oedipus's efforts to learn the cause lead him inevitably to discover the secret of his birth. In Sophocles's version of the final events, Jocasta kills herself, Oedipus puts out his eyes, leaves Thebes, and eventually perishes at Colonus.

Little wonder that the tragedy of Oedipus has sometimes been cited as a parable against adoption. Not even Philip Roth's Gregory Freytag, whom we met in Chapter 1, unleashed such havoc on his family.

Beyond that, the story of Oedipus dramatizes one of mankind's deepest fears: incest. Whether rooted in instinct or generations of culture, incest has been numbered among the primal taboos in human history. Alfred Kroeber, one of the twentieth century's most influential anthropologists, proposed years ago: "If ten anthropologists were asked to designate one universal institution, nine would likely name the incest prohibition; some have expressly named it as the only universal one."[20] And Claude Levi-Strauss argued that "the prohibition of incest can be found at the dawn of culture… [It] is culture itself."[21]

The fear of incest in turn explains the occasional resistance to adoption among many ancient and early modern societies. At least in those cases where a child of unknown parentage is brought into a family, the possibility of sexual relations between closely related persons intrudes itself. Kristin Gager quotes a seventeenth-century French jurist, Issali, who warned that confusion over identity could lead to incestuous outcomes: "Sooner or later the memory of the alienated family fades away, and once the first mistake has occurred the crime of incest will never cease."[22]

Let me suggest that the story of Oedipus does not necessarily entail a condemnation of adoption. Rather, the tragic moral lies in a warning against human pride: no mortal should try to evade the destiny decreed by the gods. Oedipus "makes a decision which springs from the deepest layer of his individual nature," and pays a terrible price.[23] Note, however, that Polybus and Merope, the adoptive parents in the tale, do not suffer for their choice. Nor is Oedipus punished for the "crime" of being abandoned and adopted. Instead, he and his family come to grief because both he and Laius, before him, defy what has been ordained.

To be sure, at least some Greeks expressed ambivalence about adoption. The loyalty and affection of adopted persons was sometimes subject to interrogation and declared deficient. Deploying adoption

DOI: 10.1057/9781137333919

metaphorically, Demosthenes distinguished indigenous Athenians from immigrants by describing the former as legitimate and the latter as merely adopted children of their country. Similarly, Lycurgus invoked adoption as an analogy in his prosecution of Leocrates for treason: "men do not hold adoptive parents in the same regard as real parents, and they feel less loyalty to countries they have adopted as well."[24]

Despite these occasional disavowals—not very different from the sorts of rhetoric I examined in Chapter 1—the practice of adoption "was commonplace in classical Greece," in W. K. Lacey's authoritative conclusion. "Adoption was not difficult," Lacey adds, "was freely practiced, and [was] recognized as entirely creditable."[25]

Indeed, while Lycurgus used adoption figuratively to demean Leocrates's patriotism, the orator Lysias made almost the opposite point in prosecuting Agoratos on a similar charge:

> In every way [Agoratas] deserves to die many times over; for the same man who says that he [was adopted] by the *demos*, the *demos*, whom he himself calls his father (*pater hautou*), [this man] is found to have injured the *demos*.... Now whoever struck his birth father (*gonoi pater*) and failed to furnish the necessities of life, and robbed his adoptive father (*poietos pater*) of all his goods, how could he not thereby deserve the death penalty according to the law against maltreatment?[26]

In short, adoption was not only a common practice but could also serve, in at least some cases, to illustrate filial loyalty.

While Greece never produced "a systematic corpus of civil law," there was a set of laws that governed adoption. The purpose of the practice was to prevent the extinction of a male lineage.[27] In classical Greece, adoption served almost exclusively to provide a man with an heir. There were three different ways of going about it: a man could adopt while he was still alive, he could nominate an heir in his will, or his surviving family could undertake a posthumous adoption. (In general, women were not permitted to adopt.)[28] The practice of adoption continued over at least six centuries (through the second century BCE), but scholars concede that the surviving records do not permit great precision in describing changes and continuity over that long period.

In most accounts, Solon is said to have legalized adoption when, in the early sixth century BCE, he promulgated the law that Athenians had the legal right to dispose of their property. That connection between adoption and property signals the most fundamental difference between Athenian adoption and the practice as we know it today. To put it briefly, in Athens

DOI: 10.1057/9781137333919

(as in most other ancient societies), adoption had nothing to do with the welfare of the adopted person—often an adult in any case—and everything to do with preserving a family's name and property intact. Adult adoptees were also expected to care for the new parent in his old age, to perform funeral ceremonies, and to carry on the parent's name and property.

In a patrilineal society, parents with one or more unmarried daughters but no sons faced a particular threat. When the father died, his daughter became an *epikleros*. The term means that she did not inherit; rather, the family property temporarily reposed with her. She was a means of conveyance, through whom property would be transferred to an acceptable (i.e., male) heir, and she was obliged to marry her father's closest male heir. In such circumstances, and to avoid that outcome, a father was legally entitled to find a husband of his choice for his daughter, then adopt the husband to avoid the alienation of his property after his death. Note that such adoptions had the effect of making the daughter's husband also her brother. In Sarah Pomeroy's comment, this form of adoption "provided for a pragmatic exception" from the strong Greek incest taboo.[29]

Adopted persons (mostly male but including some daughters) had rights that were nearly equivalent to other citizens and children. One major exception: an adopted man could not in turn adopt for any reason.

Rome

Although Roman practices were similar in many respects to those of Greece, the institution of adoption was treated with even greater respect. One scholar remarks on "the prominence and visibility of adoption within the 'best' families of Rome." Aside from ensuring the continuity of lineage, adoption could also "enable a highly controlled kind of mobility, involving either poorer relations or individuals from outside the family altogether."[30]

Typically of practices across pre-modern societies, Roman "adoption had nothing to do with the welfare of children, and those adopted were often adults."[31] Adoption was regarded as a remedy, a means of providing heirs to preserve lineage and property. For this reason, it is likely that adoption was more widespread among the upper classes; poorer families had less financial or political incentive to adopt.[32] Until 291 CE, women could not adopt; women were at that time permitted to adopt

DOI: 10.1057/9781137333919

caregivers.[33] Importantly, wives did not become the mothers of sons that their husbands adopted.

Given the purpose of adoption, as a mechanism for ensuring a father's family name and estate, adoptive sons were typically adults, rather than children. Adults had already survived the various illnesses that carried off so many Roman children. Beyond that, "the adopting father could see what he was getting as a son and heir."[34] Presumably, Roman fathers paid a price in diminished loyalty from natal children who knew that their status as heir was always provisional. In any case, the choices available to Roman fathers were embedded in what was called the *patria potestas* (the paternal control), a power that conferred a discretion that modern readers find breathtaking. Most adoptions involved members of the extended kin group.[35]

The recognition of adoption as an equivalent means of creating families may be traced in part to Roman attitudes toward sex. Most societies have insisted on the link between sexual intercourse and the exclusive legitimacy of descent: children "of the body" take precedence. This has certainly been the case across post-classical Europe, as I will discuss a little later. In contrast, in the words of one scholar,

> Roman sexuality did not create any relationship between partners; it was neither a service rendered nor a form of communication. It founded no obligation or bond on either side. In Roman society, where eating, working, going to war or living under the same roof with somebody automatically created a close relationship, sex played no such role.[36]

In addition, a newborn was not a member of the family until the child was "chosen" by the father. Those not chosen—often for reasons of deformity or apparent weakness—were abandoned, suffocated, or starved.[37] In other words, even children "of the body" were, in effect, adopted into their families.[38]

Perhaps the most famous case of Roman adoption followed from Julius Caesar's decision to name Octavian as his heir in his will. After Caesar's assassination in 44 BCE, Octavian was renamed Gaius Julius Caesar, and is known to history as "Augustus," the honorific that was awarded by the Roman Senate in 27 BCE. He reigned as Rome's first emperor for nearly forty-one years, providing exactly the stability that Julius Caesar had intended in adopting him. When Marc Antony sneered at the middling class from which Octavian/Augustus came, Cicero defended the emperor as an example of the "new men" whose energy and independence made Rome strong.[39]

DOI: 10.1057/9781137333919

The imperial precedent that Julius set was followed by many of his successors, including Augustus himself, who outlived several potential heirs and resorted to,

> a whole stream of adoptions: by himself of Tiberius, his stepson…and by Tiberius of Germanicus, who was Tiberius' patrilateral nephew ....[He] became the adoptive grandfather of the younger Drusus and of Germanicus, and therefore the potential great-grandfather of their future children.[40]

Commenting on the generally favorable estimates that historians have given to the emperors who reigned for much of the second century—Trajan, Hadrian, Antoninus Pius, and Marcus Aurelius—Nicholas Purcell speculates that part of the reason was precisely that they were chosen rather than ascending to the purple through inheritance. To be sure, these men were often kinsmen of their predecessors, but none was "in direct of line of descent and [each] was chosen by adoption…as son and heir."[41] In short, selection as heir by the emperor could be seen as a sign of merit rather than elevation through the sheer randomness of biological descent.

Like the Mesopotamian real estate tycoon in Nuzi, Romans sometimes used adoption for political purposes, and with startling opportunism. The most famous instance concerns Clodius, a patrician and major political figure who, around 60 BCE, wanted to become officially a plebian—to "de-class" himself, as Orwell might say—in order to secure a tribunate reserved for men in that rank. He renounced his patrician rank, had himself adopted by a pleb, and took office as a plebian tribune. The adoption, abetted by Julius Caesar, was almost certainly illegal. Among other irregularities, the man who adopted Clodius was younger than he was, while Roman adoption law demanded that the adoptive parent be at least fifteen years older. Cicero launched a savage attack on the adoption, accusing Clodius of "subverting" the sacred rites "polluting" families. Above all, according to Cicero, Clodius has "set nature at defiance," a charge that demonstrates how malleable the term "nature" can be.[42]

These Roman examples illustrate again that family relationships show considerable variability across time and culture. To return to the question I raised in Chapter 1 of this book, one scholar has proposed "the frequency of adoption is yet another proof that nature played little part in the Roman conception of the family." A child was given in adoption in the same way that a daughter was given in marriage.[43] Indeed, in "many non-European societies, birth and biological relationships are not essential

DOI: 10.1057/9781137333919

to the definition of kinship. On the contrary, kinship may be established on the basis of performance and conduct, in which case what one does outweighs what one is by birth."[44]

China

Before following the story of adoption into post-classical Europe let me turn briefly to the case of China and India, the two ancient Asian civilizations that have left the most abundant records relating to adoption.[45]

The *Analects* of Confucius (ca. 500 BCE) codified the patriarchal, patrilinear norms that would guide Chinese society for the next 2500 years. Because the cult of ancestral veneration was even stronger in imperial China than in early Western societies, the need for an heir was felt with special anxiety. The combination of infertility and high rates of mortality created the linked problems of threatening the survival of a family's name and the survival of its property. In addition to that, a father wanted care in his old age and reverence for himself and his ancestors after death.

Early imperial literature contained objections to adoption—Mencius, for example, wrote that "Heaven gives birth to creatures in such a way that they only have one root," and the text was understood to endorse strict biological lines of descent. Far more typically, however, pragmatism prevailed; China accepted and even encouraged adoption to create or recreate viable lines of succession. A similar sense of practicality defined the pool of potential adoptees: the rules stipulated that only those with the same surname were eligible, but violations of those rules occurred constantly, as men enlarged the pool in search of suitable adoptive sons.

Ann Waltner suggests that the term "adoption" can refer to several related but different Chinese practices. The most common, and closest to Western practice, was the legal act of bringing a male relative into a family to inherit and to take responsibility for ritual memorial obligations. Because adopted sons bore serious obligations, young children were typically not considered acceptable candidates, and infant adoption was quite rare.[46]

Various terms for adoption also referred to less formal arrangements, for instance the adoption of soldiers by their general or even subjects by the emperor. In one famous instance, during the early sixteenth century, the emperor Wuzong "adopted" 127 men in one day. His apparent purpose was to bind their loyalty more tightly by conferring quasi-familial status.[47] In short, adoption in some cases served as legal fact and in other cases as a non-binding symbol of affiliation.

DOI: 10.1057/9781137333919

The key point is that the "prominence given to notions of blood affinity in early modern Europe has no Chinese counterpart."[48] Confucian notions of patriarchy and patrilineal descent coexisted quite comfortably with the improvisations of adoptive kinship. As long as an adequate male heir was found, families could look forward with confidence to generational continuity.

In this respect at least, the Chinese resembled the Romans, for whom adoption provided a fully acceptable instrument for preserving a family's name and possessions. Like the Romans, too, the Chinese practiced posthumous adoption. If a man died without descendants to provide the offerings, "a brother usually assigned one of his sons to the deceased's line. The adoption was effected by writing a contract on a red sheet of paper, which was then inserted under the base of the dead man's tablet."[49] In exchange for the memorial services he performed, the adopted son became eligible to inherit a portion of the dead man's estate.

The primary focus of adoption was "always the family and family line, the men in the household and their patrilineal ancestors and descendants."[50] It appears that these attitudes about adoption prevailed for centuries. According one scholar, the acquisition of designated (or "ritual") heirs can be traced from the Han (202 BCE–22 CE) through the Qing (1644–1911), a period of over 2000 years.

If more recent practice is a guide to the past, it appears that adopted sons were easily assimilated into their new families and villages. This despite the fact that adoptive transactions frequently involved men and boys who had been sold by their former parents. "Taking late imperial China as a whole," Myron Cohen has written, "it is well known that men, women, and children could be sold"; they were considered "commodities."[51]

Despite the general acceptance of adoption, on at least one occasion, in the early 1520s, a dispute over adoption threatened to topple a dynasty. The episode, sometimes called "the Great Ritual Controversy," tested the legitimacy of three generations of the imperial family. Before his death in 1521, the heirless Wuzong—the same Wuzong who adopted his soldiers—named the teenage prince of Xing, the son of Wuzong's elder brother, to succeed him as Shizong. However, following the death of Wuzong, court officials asked Shizong to take the title of heir-apparent, rather than emperor, which he refused. To put it simply, Shizong insisted on being the son of his dead father, rather than the son of the deceased emperor. To achieve this, he demanded that his father be given posthumous

DOI: 10.1057/9781137333919

imperial rank. Three years of quite bitter wrangling ensued, at the end of which 230 officials descended on the palace, pounding on the gates and demanding Shizong's cooperation. Instead, he had 134 of them arrested, seventeen of whom subsequently died of their punishments.[52] For his part, Shizong ruled, under the reign name Jiajing, for forty-five years.

In short, even in cultures that have embraced adoption more or less fully—several earlier emperors of China had reached the throne through adoption—the practice has frequently carried a burden of potential misgiving.

India

It is almost certainly the case that India presents the most complicated example of adoption law and practice in any society, ancient or modern. To begin with, sonship is divided into twelve different kinds in Hindu legal texts, a set of filial arrangements that have been called "the most striking feature of Indian family law."[53] The inventory of sonship includes the legitimate son (*aurasa*), the son of an appointed daughter (*putrika putra*), the son born secretly (*gudhaja*), the son bought (*kritaka*), the son cast-off (*apaviddha*), the son by a concubine (*parasava*), and half-a-dozen others, including the adopted son (*dattaka*).

Adoption is by turns forbidden or approved along literally scores of kinship relations. As in Rome and China, preference in adoption was given to the closest male relative. Finally, while most texts endorse adoption, some (the Rigveda) oppose it, and others are silent. One of the most eminent authorities on ancient and medieval civil law in India describes adoption as a place of "bewildering confusion."[54]

John Mayne's *Treatise on Hindu Law and Usage* (1878), which includes a chapter of 100 pages on adoption, remains the starting point for all studies of this subject. Arguing that religion and inheritance both guided the practice of Hindu adoption, Mayne quotes a Baudhayana rite which includes the words, "I take thee for the fulfillment of religious duties. I take thee to continue the line of my ancestors."[55]

Insofar as any generalization is possible across such variation, the practice was embedded in worldly as well as spiritual aspirations. Later scholars have agreed with Mayne that adoption was practiced in all regions of India, and among all classes.[56] While early legendary texts record more adoptions of daughters than sons, historical practice has reinforced patrilinear

DOI: 10.1057/9781137333919

descent: men adopted other men and boys as sons and heirs. Preference was given to individuals who were related to the prospective parent, though cases of more distant kinship, or none, have been recorded.

According to Mayne, an "orphan cannot be validly adopted, in the absence of a custom to the contrary," and such customs were rare.[57] This provision, which seems almost counter-intuitive to a modern reader, merely emphasizes once again the pragmatic purpose of adoption that prevailed in older societies, in which the chief motive was preservation of lineage and property.

Post-classical Rome and the European Middle Ages

By the end of the fourth century, the Roman Empire had divided in half, the West being ruled from Rome and Ravenna, the East from Constantinople, which Constantine had founded in 330 CE on the site of Byzantium. Within 200 years, the Western Empire collapsed—476 CE is the date given in textbooks, with misleading precision—while the Eastern Empire, called the Byzantine Empire from about the sixth century, survived for another 1000 years.

In both halves of the empire, life remained hard for most people, hardest for unwanted or orphaned children. James O'Donnell has provided a glimpse of daily life in sixth-century Italy, reconstructing the mid-September market festival that took place every year in a town called Consolinum. In this immense gathering of merchants, peddlers, beggars, thieves, aristocrats, traveling musicians, and religious enthusiasts—"a veritable city without buildings"—everything was for sale. Along with agricultural produce, livestock, jewelry, and textiles, the festival hosted "a brisk trade in children whose impoverished parents sold them into slavery."[58]

In the Eastern Empire, adoption was at least an option. While adoption is not mentioned in Warren Treadgold's comprehensive, 1000-page *History of the Byzantine State and Society* (1997), it has been a relatively prominent subject in more specialized studies of the Byzantine Empire. It appears that, in the matter of adoption, the Byzantines adhered to Roman legal precedent, permitting adoption and surrounding the practice with rules and procedures. A typical contract, dating from the year 554, recounts that a widowed mother declared that she could not afford to take care of her nine-year-old daughter and was therefore giving her

DOI: 10.1057/9781137333919

to another couple "on condition that they adopt her as their own child." Such contracts can be found as early as the fourth century and as late as the twelfth.[59] Leo VI, a ninth-century emperor, codified an ecclesiastical blessing appropriate to adoption. And significantly, several adoption stories are found in lives of saints.[60]

These bits of evidence suggest that the practice carried some spiritual advantage. Even greater benefits attached to those laypersons who were taken into a monastic family by "spiritual adoption."[61] This allocation of religious merit followed from the declaration of a church council in 692 that "spiritual kinship was superior to kinship of the flesh."[62] In short, adoption was widely practiced within the theological framework of Eastern Christianity.

The story of adoption is completely different in the West. Adoption more or less disappeared in Europe in the fifteen centuries that followed the fall of Rome. In the words of Jack Goody, the most influential student of this history, "the disappearance was remarkably abrupt."[63] Given the prominent position of adoption in Roman law and society, and the long-term influence of Roman legal precedents on subsequent European statutes, the quite sudden erasure of adoption seems at first glance all the more puzzling.

Following scholars such as Fritz Schultz and P. D. King, Goody observes that the early legislative codes of the Germans and Celts and other Romanized peoples in the West contain virtually no references to adoption. Nor do the Visigothic Codes of Spain, which are otherwise strongly inflected by Roman precedent.[64]

Imperial and ecclesiastical authorities collaborated in suppressing adoption. In the sixth century, Justinian's *Institutes*, about one quarter of which dealt with questions of succession and inheritance, had made adoption more difficult. Justinian placed several new restrictions on who could adopt, who could be adopted, and what steps had to be taken to ensure legality.[65] However, while these laws might have reduced somewhat the number of adoptions, they would not have eliminated the practice.

How and why did adoption disappear? Goody's explanation lies in the power of the Christian church, which "effectively prevented [adoption] for fifteen hundred years."[66] Adoption, never explicitly forbidden, was vociferously discouraged, in terms that emphasized God's disapproval of the practice.

Throughout the ancient world, as we have seen, adoption was primarily a strategy through which men provided heirs for their names and property.

DOI: 10.1057/9781137333919

At some point, the leaders of the Church realized that the Church itself could become the beneficiaries of men who died without heirs. As Goody puts it, the results of disappearance of adoption were "clear enough." The Church could profit from death of childless, heirless married persons. In short, "the Church could only benefit by excluding 'fictional' heirs."

By the fifth and sixth centuries, the Church had become what it has remained to this day: a Big Business. Every potential source of revenue had to be expanded and fully exploited and new sources had to be continuously under development. Deploying its coercive power, which reached into the most intimate details of personal life, Church leaders mobilized every theological resource to discourage any strategy that might stand between its treasury and the income represented by the deaths of men and women without heirs.

Recall that the Middle Ages were as dangerous as the preceding classical era had been: the whole point of adoption had been precisely to find a mechanism for coping with the high death rates that disease and injury inflicted as a matter of course on individuals of all classes and ages. Christianity changed all that: "No longer, as in Cicero's time, could a man's fictional heir keep alive the worship of his family; oblations [i.e., testamentary gifts to the clergy] placed this responsibility in the hands of the Church. The take-over of the worship of ancestors was also a take-over of their inheritance."[67]

One of the chief actors in the Christian campaign against adoption was a fifth-century writer named Salvian. Like his slightly older contemporary Augustine, Salvian lived amid the decline of the Roman Empire. The years he devoted to the search for an explanation led to his major work, a treatise *On the Government of God*. However, he figures in our story because of another work, *Against Avarice*, in which he warns those who have no children that adoption insults God's providential planning. Adoption is, in effect, a crime against God and—here we go again— against nature. Salvian even commands that parents who do have children should disinherit them. Better poverty in this life and prosperity in the next.

With a similar logic, passages in the New Testament that appear to sanction adoption had to be re-interpreted. In Romans 8:14–17, Paul tells his readers:

> For as many as are led by the Spirit of God, they are the sons of God.
>
> For ye have not received the spirit of bondage again to fear; but ye have received the Spirit of adoption, whereby we cry, Abba, Father.

DOI: 10.1057/9781137333919

> The Spirit itself beareth witness with our spirit, that we are the children of God:
>
> And if children, then heirs; heirs of God, and joint-heirs with Christ; if so be that we suffer with him, that we may be also glorified together.

Theologians artfully insisted that "adoption" (and heirship) here must be understood as exclusively spiritual and metaphorical: it was fine for God to adopt his chosen, but the practice must not be extended to human relationships. Families must be built only in "way of nature," through sexual intercourse and birth. Adoptive parents were replaced by "godparents," who bore a strictly religious responsibility for their godchildren. Children could not legitimately take a legal place in families other than those of their birth. This prejudice was reinforced by a pious fear that Christian orphans might be adopted by non-Christian families.[68]

England provides an illuminating case study of adoption's long absence in Europe. Adoption did not exist in British common law, and was not legalized by statute until 1926. Adoption is mentioned only once in the great compendium that Pollock and Maitland assembled under the title *History of English Law* (1895), and is not mentioned at all in the thirteen volumes of Sir William Holdsworth's *The History of English Law* (1909).[69]

In part this was the result of longstanding ecclesiastical opposition. But in equal or greater part, the absence of adoption reflected a powerful aristocratic devotion to blood ties. Under the rules of primogeniture, property and titles passed from father to eldest son, and to the nearest male kin if no son was living. Inheritance could not be assigned by choice. As one writer summarizes the position:

> The primitive understanding of adoption required the adoptee to become a member of the adopter's family, to acquire a quasi-interest in the adopter's property while the latter lived and to succeed to such property upon the adopter's death. But to the English, heirs meant legitimate children who were heirs of the blood.[70]

The idea that anyone should succeed to title or property other than legitimate male heirs was "repugnant to English society."[71] This position, which governed English laws of succession for at least 600 years, had been given definitive expression in the twelfth century by Ranulf de Glanville, Edward II's justiciar (roughly, chief minister). In the legal code attributed to him, Ranulf declares that "Only God can make a *heres*

DOI: 10.1057/9781137333919

[heir], not man."[72] Adoption in such cases was not merely discouraged but forbidden.

In *Utopia* (1516), Thomas More described an imaginary world of adoption, specifically to provide greater freedom for (male) children who wanted to pursue a trade other than their fathers:

> As a rule, the son is trained to his father's craft, for which most feel a natural inclination. But if anyone is attracted to another occupation, he is transferred by adoption into a family practicing the trade he prefers.[73]

In the non-fictional world, however, adoption was forbidden. What was true for ordinary Englishmen was also true for the king, as this exchange in Shakespeare's *3 Henry VI* suggests. Henry argues that his kingship rests rightly on two bases, that he is heir by blood to Henry IV and Henry V, and that Henry IV in turn was heir by adoption to Richard II:

> K. Henry. Tell me, may not a king adopt an heir?
>
> York. What then?
>
> K. Hen. And if he may, then am I lawful king;
>
> For Richard, in the view of many lords,
>
> Resign'd the crown to Henry the Fourth,
>
> Whose heir my father was, and I am his. (I, i, 135–140)

Exeter objects to Henry's claim on two counts. First, he repeats Warwick's claim that Richard gave up his crown to Henry IV only under coercion. Exeter's more serious rebuttal is that an adopted son cannot come between an heir and his inheritance:

> ...he could not so resign his crown
>
> But that the next heir should succeed and reign. (145–146)

From Ranulf de Glanville to Fielding and Dickens: one student of adoption's history has suggested, "It is because of this special emphasis on blood that British literature is full of wards, guardians, foundlings, and illegitimate sons."[74]

In the absence of adoption, the English employed a number of alternatives to care for—or at least dispose of—the orphaned and homeless. These included "placing out" and apprenticeships, practices that were transported to the New England colonies in the seventeenth century. Such procedures supposedly "made adoption for social welfare purposes unnecessary."[75] In fact, of course, that idea was either utopian or cynical: children were routinely abused by these arrangements, an outcome that

DOI: 10.1057/9781137333919

brought increasing discomfort to English policy makers in the eighteenth and nineteenth centuries.

One other European example. Historically, France had been counted among the countries most energetically opposed to adoption. In her splendid history of adoption in France, Kristin Gager quotes several relevant opinions. A sixteenth-century jurist named Charles Dumoulin condemned adoption as a challenge to the "natural" order of things: "those who wish that their name live forever after them rise up against God himself as well as against the vicissitudes of Nature ..." Another jurist, Claude Henrys, insisted that "Adoptions were abolished a long time ago, not only by our own traditions and customary law, but by the general law of Christianity, as St. Justin Martyr and Tertullian remarked in their *Apologies*. This is because adoptions run not only against the demands of nature, but also against the precepts of the Gospel...."[76] We have heard these self-serving appeals to nature before, here again used to enforce a purely elective discipline.

Despite this loud chorus of disapproval, Gager finds evidence that adoption did take place, at least in some French regions some of the time. And less formal adoptions are also recorded. Consider the case of the prominent writer, Anna Leatitia Barbauld. In 1775, apparently concerned that she and her husband could not have children, she made the following remarkable proposal to her brother, the physician John Aitkin:

> Our request then, in short, is this: that you will permit us to adopt one of your children; which of them, we leave to you;—that you will make it ours in every sense in which it is possible to make it,—that you will transfer to us all the care and all the authority of a parent; that we should provide for it, educate it, and have the entire direction of it as far into life as the parental power itself extends.
>
> I am sensible it is not a small thing we ask; nor can it be easy for a parent to part with a child. This I would say, from a number, one may more easily be spared. Though it makes a very material difference in happiness whether a person has children or no children, it makes, I apprehend, little or none whether he has three, or four; five, or six; because four or five are enow to exercise all his whole stock of care and affection.[77]

Whether or not Dr. Aitkin agreed with his sister's rather daffy quantitative analysis, he did agree to transfer his son Charles to her permanent keeping.

The details of this "adoption" may have been distinctive, but the transfer of a child from one family to another was surely not unusual.

DOI: 10.1057/9781137333919

Nonetheless, in general, adoption in a more formal, legal sense became an uncommon practice in the years following the ascendancy of the Christian Church in Europe.

At the same time, orphaned and abandoned children may have fared better under the familial rules enforced by the Church than they had in classical antiquity. To begin with, as we have seen, adoption in the ancient world had nothing to do with the welfare of children and everything to do with securing heirs. In addition, infanticide, which was a relatively common occurrence in Egypt and Greece, was also "a familiar phenomenon" throughout the Roman Empire: it was "an ordinary part of existence."[78] It was inflicted on many children who were neither deformed nor illegitimate, and more frequently on girls than boys.

The Church outlawed infanticide, which "was deemed an offense against God and the family, and included in the group of crimes considered especially heinous such as witchcraft, heresy, and incest."[79] The practice nonetheless continued, at least occasionally and perhaps more frequently: Barbara Kellum has, for example, reported on infanticide in medieval England.[80] At the same time, the decline in adoptions in medieval Europe was matched by a corresponding increase in both formal and informal care for foundlings and orphans. The first foundling hospitals were opened in the fourteenth century, in Italy, and the institution quickly spread across Europe.

In earlier centuries, some children had circulated among families through a widespread custom of calculated abandonment. That is the conclusion John Boswell reached in *The Kindness of Strangers*, the title of which suggests his thesis. Abandonment appears to have been widespread across all of pre-modern Europe: as many as thirty or even forty percent of children may have experienced this fate.[81] The practice was so commonplace that Clement of Alexandria commanded fathers to stay away from prostitutes (whether male or female) because they might commit inadvertent incest.

In Boswell's view, historians have frequently but mistakenly conflated abandonment with infanticide. On the contrary, abandonment had in many cases precisely the opposite purpose. To ensure that the abandoned children would be found, they were typically left in public places: secured to tree branches (out of the reach of animals), wrapped and placed in baskets in well-traveled fields, or left at intersections. Following protocols that were familiar though not usually written down, families would know when and where to look for these children.

DOI: 10.1057/9781137333919

In short, families with too many children used abandonment to transfer one or more of those children to families who needed them. In other instances, particularly among the upper classes, children were given to monasteries and other religious houses: an "oblation" which provided protection for the child, recruits or servants for religious establishments, and spiritual credit for the parents. The custom was so widely understood that revolving stone shelves were frequently built into abbey and monastery walls. Parents who had decided to turn over a child to a religious order would place the baby on the stone shelf, ring a bell, and depart. One of the monastery personnel would move the shelf to the inside and take the baby; the mechanics of the device ensured that neither party to the transaction could see the other. The child would typically spend the rest of its life in the service of that order.

I can only speculate about the feelings such parents may have had when they watched their child disappear behind monastery walls. Here I will talk about my own feelings. In the early 1980s, when Jennifer was about ten years old, Terry and I and our four children spent a week travelling in the English countryside. Blessed by fine weather, we picnicked in the fields, slept in bed and breakfasts, and visited every church and old town we could find. One day, walking around the walls of a ruined abbey, we encountered a stone shelf still intact. We debated the purpose of this odd device (John Boswell's book still lay in my future) and came up with several alternatives: prayerful notes and gifts for the monks or late-night deliveries of produce were among the choices. It was Jennifer who suggested that perhaps babies had been moved inside in this way. For a few minutes, the six of us simply stood and looked at that wall, with curiosity and sorrow.

The good news here, if Boswell is right, is that children who were transferred into private homes and religious institutions experienced mortality rates that were not significantly higher than for other children.[82] Indeed, in his book's concluding chapter, he documents the tragically high death rates recorded in late medieval foundling hospitals, designed to be places of humanitarian refuge, but proving in fact to be hotbeds of communicable diseases. Abandonment, in this reading, offered children a far better chance of survival than institutional care.

So far, this chapter has offered a survey of adoption in the ancient and medieval worlds, in both Europe and Asia. I want to conclude with a brief and highly selective review of modern laws and practices.

DOI: 10.1057/9781137333919

Over the past 200 years, the concept of adoption has been profoundly transformed. As we have seen, in virtually all ancient societies for which evidence can be found, the foremost purpose of adoption was to provide an heir. Whether to ensure the continuation of a family name, or to secure the descent of property rights, or to provide for funeral memorials, adoption was intended to serve the needs of adult adopters. Today, it is universally the case that adoption is understood to serve the needs of children.

How and when did that fundamental re-orientation come about? For the past half-century, historians have been engaged in a lively (sometimes fevered) debate over the "discovery" or the "invention" of childhood. The text that launched this undertaking was *Centuries of Childhood*, published in French in 1960 and translated into English two years later. According to Philip Ariès, in what may be the most frequently quoted sentence in the book: "in medieval society, the idea of childhood did not exist."[83] He argues that only gradually and progressively, from the seventeenth century, did European society begin to formulate a concept of childhood as a separate and special sphere.

Ariès's thesis has come under attack since the day of its publication, for its data, its chronology, its assumptions, and its alleged confusions of fictional and non-fictional sources. We can skip the details of the controversy. This much is undeniable: whether modern conceptions of childhood were invented or evolved by imperceptible degrees, social legislation specifically directed toward the welfare of children has been a product of the modern era. Beginning in the eighteenth century, and with gathering force in the 200 years since, parliaments around the developed world have enacted laws aimed at protecting children: from domestic neglect and abuse, from dangerous employment, from sexual trafficking.[84]

I would advance the claim that the concept of modernity itself is bound up with our concern for the protection of children. This is the larger cultural and legal context that has corresponded with the transformation of adoption from a mechanism for inheritance into an instrument of child welfare. Today, outside the Islamic nations, almost every country in the world has accepted adoption as a proper and legal practice, and has enacted laws that govern it. A half-dozen examples will suffice.

In France, the Code Napoleon (1804) did include provision for adoption, but only in cases where the person adopting was at least

DOI: 10.1057/9781137333919

fifty and had neither children nor legitimate descendants. The person adopted had to be at least fifteen years younger than the prospective parent, and had to have received care for at least six years. France legislated more spacious adoption procedures only in 1923, after the First World War and the lethal influenza epidemic that followed, in response to horrific family disruptions that produced a generation of orphans.

The British Parliament passed an adoption statute in 1926, also in the wake of the war and the influenza epidemic that had carried off tens of thousands of parents, many of them young. However, agitation toward legalized adoption had begun a century earlier, as part of a growing humanitarian concern for children's welfare. Wordsworth and Dickens and other writers and reformers had instructed their countrymen in the value and the vulnerability of children. At the same time, the Industrial Revolution condemned tens of thousands of children to the dangers of punishing labor and unsanitary home conditions.

In one scholar's summary of this dismal episode in British history "orphans and paupers were sent to industrial areas and, in order to meet the labor demand, were forced into factory work by the state."[85]

Writing in the early 1950s, an English writer looked back indignantly on the centuries of child abuse that had ultimately provoked reforms that included adoption:

> ... for 350 years or so—from Henry the Eighth's first Poor Law in 1530—the problem of the unwanted child solved itself in three ways, through child labour and the poorhouse apprentice, through infant mortality, and through baby-farming of the grossest kind. Society might be worried about the morals of the parents, but not about the disposal of the hundreds of thousands of children spewed into the gutters every year. These died or paid their way.[86]

Other Anglophone countries also embraced adoption in the years around the turn of the twentieth century. New Zealand passed its first adoption legislation in 1881, which was designed, in the words of an early analysis, both "for the benefit of the adopted child" and to provide "a more effective scope for the philanthropic activities of kindly disposed people."[87] In Australia, adoption is governed by each State and Territory. The first such ordinance, the Western Australia Adoption of Children Act, was passed in 1896. Other states followed, and all the states adopted

DOI: 10.1057/9781137333919

uniform codes in the mid-1960s.[88] Canadian law recognized adoption in the 1920s. As in Australia, adoption is regulated at the provincial level; the first law was passed in 1921 in Ontario.

Following the legal changes in France, adoption was gradually regularized across Western Europe. In 1967, Italian law was reformed to permit adoption of children up to the age of 8, and to lower the minimum age for the adoptive parent from fifty years to thirty-five. Even then, however, "the adoption of adults was still considered the standard (and was thus called 'ordinary adoption'), while the adoption of children was called 'special adoption.'"[89] West Germany enacted modern adoption laws in 1977.

Spain legalized adoption in 1987. According to the EU memorandum on the subject, expanded opportunities for adoption was supported not only by advocates of children's welfare, but also by opponents of abortion. Even in the new adoption regime, the process takes an average of nine years.[90]

An earlier adoption law, promulgated by Franco's fascist regime in 1941, made it legal to insert the names of adoptive parents as biological parents on birth certificates. The law's purpose was to erase the connection between children and persons who were judged to be enemies of the state. Beginning with the end of the Spanish Civil War in 1939, tens of thousands of anti-fascists were executed or imprisoned; their children were handed over to loyal Falangist families and institutions. This totalitarian practice continued for decades throughout the postwar period, long after the fascists had lost power. All together, hundreds of thousands of babies were stolen from their mothers by Catholic nuns, priests, and doctors and sold, initially to supporters of Franco's fascist regime, later to whoever was the highest bidder.

After giving birth, mothers would be told that their babies—babies that had seemed quite healthy—had died. Women who asked to see their dead infants were refused permission. In fact, with the connivance of church and government, thousands of these girls and boys were simply sold to interested men and women willing to pay the equivalent of hundreds and even thousands of dollars. In the course of exposing the barbaric practice, many of the infant graves that were opened revealed coffins with piles of stones, or bones of adults.[91] The infants who were stolen from their birth mothers were effectively kidnapped, not adopted.

An even more repugnant version of this story comes from Guatemala. During the thirty-six years of that country's brutal civil war, from 1960 to 1996, the government murdered upwards of 180,000 men,

DOI: 10.1057/9781137333919

women, and children. In the spring of 2012, Oscar Ramirez was living in Framingham, Massachusetts when he received a phone call from a prosecutor in Guatemala. Ramirez, 31 years old, had emigrated to the U.S. a dozen years earlier. He believed that his mother had died when he was a baby, and that his father had died in a truck accident when he was four. His grandmother had raised him, and his memories of his childhood were happy.

Eventually, Ramirez learned that the dead man he had cherished in his memory for over two decades was not his father. He had in fact been part of an army murder detail that had killed almost everyone in a little town called Dos Erres. Infant Oscar had been spared and abducted by one of the murderers, who renamed him and incorporated him into his family. That revelation was followed by another: Ramirez's 70-year-old father, Tranquilo Castenada, was among the few townspeople who escaped the massacre. Driven nearly insane by the deaths of his entire family—he knew nothing of Oscar's fate—Castenada spent the next three decades living on his own in the jungle. Father and son were re-united on May 31, 2012.[92]

Today, as in ancient Israel, adoption "is not known as a legal institution in Jewish law."[93] At the same time, the law does make provision for the physical and financial care of an orphaned child by an adult guardian. The outcome is nearly identical to adoption with the reservation that family membership is not encompassed by the arrangement. Even inheritance, which is customarily limited to birth children, can be arranged through explicit testamentary documents. In short, while adoption has not had legal sanction in Jewish law, adoption *de facto* has remained a viable option for families and children.

Nearly equivalent to adoption, the provision for guardianship is authorized by texts such as this from the Talmud: "Whoever raises an orphan in his home, scripture considers him as he gave birth to the child."[94] Not all Jewish branches permit adoption. The Lubavitch movement has stated its opposition to formal legal adoption, "on the grounds that parents kiss their children, and if the Hasid and his wife adopt children they may be guilty of the sin of kissing members of the opposite sex to whom they are not related by blood."[95]

The modern state of Israel has enacted laws governing adoption of children (most recently in 1981), which permit both domestic and international adoption under certain circumstances. Interestingly, Israel had

DOI: 10.1057/9781137333919

to adapt an old term, *ametz*, to describe adoption because there was no word for adoption in classical Hebrew.[96] While reaffirming the integrity of the family unit as a religious and societal goal, current Israeli practice also consults the "best interests of the child," a standard that, as we will see, was developed in Europe and the United States in the nineteenth century and has since become an international standard.

Adoptive practices differ widely across the countries and regions of Africa. Women in East Cameroon, according to one scholar, use foster-age to strengthen to enlarge and strengthen family networks. Childless women among the Maasi of East Africa are ritually connected with the children of other mothers in order to retain their place in the continuity of the group. In Aud Talle's striking summation, "Just as calves can be fostered by other cows in the herd…so children can be connected to women in the patrilinear family other than their biological mothers. As one herd, so also one family."

And in Northern Benin, to quote the title of an essay on the subject, "The real parents are the foster parents." I wish I had known that three decades ago, when Jennifer told me I was not her "real" father.[97]

In Asia, despite a long and deeply embedded commitment to genetic kinship, adoption has made legal progress. Throughout most of the modern era, Korean families only took in children who were relatively close kin. While formal adoption did not exist, one study concluded that the number of adopted sons among heirs increased from the fifteenth to the twentieth centuries, and that by the time of the Japanese occupation in 1910, three out of ten family successors were adopted.[98]

The shift from informal to formal adoption followed the Korean War (1950–1953), in which upwards of 6 million people were killed or died from injuries, disease, or starvation. Another 5 million men, women, and children became refugees. The humanitarian crisis in the South overwhelmed orphanages, leading to an upsurge in the number of abandoned children. In 1960, after seven years of debate, adoption was legalized. While the practice is still shadowed by traditional cultural suspicion, and the numbers remain quite small, domestic adoptions have steadily increased over the past half-century.[99]

Early modern adoption in Japan was usually associated with the efforts of second (or third) sons to improve their economic chances. "Adoption rules were flexible," enabling some mobility within a fairly rigid class structure. A son, for example, might be adopted and made heir to the property of a sonless farmer. Or a warrior might adopt the daughter of a

DOI: 10.1057/9781137333919

merchant to make her eligible for marriage with another warrior; this in turn would raise the merchant's prestige.[100]

The story of adoption in postwar Japan has followed two wildly divergent scripts. On the one hand, the number of adoptions has increased dramatically. In one survey, 30 percent of respondents indicated that their relatives included at least one adopted person—a level matched only by the United States. However, the details underneath these raw statistics present an unsettling mixture of motives. Along with whatever quantity of altruism may at work, three other reasons have been proposed for the high rate of adoption: adoption of sons-in-law, adoption of extramarital lovers, and adoption to reduce taxes.[101] Furthermore, most of the adoptees in these categories are adults. Of 90,000 adoptions completed in Japan in 1985, only one-third were children, and fewer than three percent involved the adoption of a minor child by an unrelated adult. In some respects, in other words, with respect to adoption, modern Japan more closely resembles the older practices of East and West than the rest of the developed world in the twentieth and twenty-first centuries.

At the same time, the adoption of children from orphanages lags woefully behind. According to one account, in March 2011, 36,450 children were housed in Japanese orphanages. In 2010, only 4,373—about 12%—were adopted or placed in foster care. The country's many orphanages are a legacy of the devastation Japan's families suffered in the war. They have become, in a pernicious way, embedded in the culture. Thus, the majority of the boys and girls who reside in these institutions have living parents, who have placed them in orphanages for any number of reasons and who do not, under Japanese law, have to surrender their parental rights. The children may remain in these facilities until their eighteenth birthday.[102]

Adoption in post-war China has been substantially shaped by the influence of the 1979 one-child policy. Stated briefly, the policy restricts couples to one child, with exceptions for minority families and for rural families whose first child was a girl. The rule was intended to slow population growth and thus lighten the burden of an economy just beginning to emerge from poverty. At the same time, the policy conflicted with traditional attitudes that placed high value on large families including at least one son. In some cases, women are using adoption to evade the one-child policy.

The first national adoption law, which was enacted in 1992, required that adoptive parents be childless, thirty-five years old, and capable of providing

DOI: 10.1057/9781137333919

for a child's physical and educational needs. Aligned with the one-child policy, the law has contributed to the rising number of legal adoptions. The overall rate of adoption doubled in the years after 1979: from fewer than 200,000 in the 1970s to 500,000 in 1987—this despite laws in some provinces that bar women with children from adopting at all.[103]

The policy has had some unpredictable consequences for girls. Because of the lower status of females in Chinese society, the one-child regime has caused an increase in sex-selective abortion, and a larger incidence of abandonment.[104] At the same time, girls are more often adopted than boys, simply because more girls are available to families seeking children. This remains true for both Chinese and foreign parents seeking adoptive children (a subject to which I will return in Chapter 4).

One scholar has estimated that in the 1980s and 1990s, 3 to 4% of girls in China were given up for adoption. Almost all of them were adopted into Chinese families, often families with sons. Judged by school enrollment and other indicators, many of these girls have not been treated well. They are often used to provide domestic service, and "possibly to hedge parents of sons against future bride shortages (there is a long tradition of such adoptions in China)."[105]

According to one source, in the years before and following the Second World War, many Taiwanese condemned the adoption of girls as daughters because of a belief that adopted girls were frequently sold into prostitution. While that motivation cannot be proved, "it is nonetheless true that a very large percentage of prostitutes and other female entertainers were adopted daughters."[106]

Muslim countries have not in general accepted adoption. Two verses of the Quran, Sura 33, 5 and 37, have been understood to prohibit adoption. Believers are commanded to preserve blood ties as the exclusive path to the creation of family ties. In pre-Islamic Arabia, adoption had been permitted, for the same reasons we have seen in other ancient societies: the incorporation of an heir. According to the *Encyclopedia of Islam*, the prohibition of adoption "is no doubt more easily understood if it is remembered that Islam regards the 'natural' nuclear family, rather than the tribe, as the basis of the community (*umma*)."[107] Adoption can thus be seen as disruptive, a threat to the integrity of lineages.

Tunisia is the only Arab Muslim country that has enacted laws permitting adoption in the full sense that creates filiation and equality

DOI: 10.1057/9781137333919

of inheritance. At the same time, while it forbids adoption, the Quran expressly commends the care of orphans. These children should be valued, protected, and treated in all respects except name and inheritance as a non-adoptive son or daughter.[108] Thus, *kafalah* is the model proposed by Sharia law in this respect.

The rejection of adoption also defines policy in the Muslim countries of sub-Saharan Africa. Elsewhere on the continent, adoption was a regular feature of kinship structures, though often in patterns quite different from European models. According to Jack Goody, the differences between hoe culture, which predominated in tropical Africa, and the plough culture of Europe brought distinctive differences in inheritance and adoption.

Let me conclude this selective review of adoption policy and practice with the case of Oceania. Studies of adoption in the South Pacific have a long history, in part because the many societies of the region appealed to anthropology's keen interest in comparative kinship, especially among cultures that anthropologists used to call "primitive."

Vern Carroll's book, *Adoption in Eastern Oceania*, collects studies across a dozen or so different island groups, and contains a useful assortment of observations on the many varieties of adoption in the South Pacific. The societies included range from Hawaii and the Society Islands in Eastern Polynesia to Nukuoro and Kapingamarangi in Western Polynesia, from the Gilbert Islands to Truk in Micronesia.

From the diverse reports, it appears that there has been an "extremely high incidence" of adoption in many parts of Oceania. Unusual levels of infertility offer one explanation. In addition, some couples with one or more sons or daughters feel a desire for more children than fertility will provide: in other words, "childlessness" may be a frame of mind rather than a simple demographic fact. On some Pacific islands, "only older sons and daughters were expected to marry, whereas younger sons and daughters were expected to be satisfied to adopt their older siblings' surplus offspring."

Because of the great diversity of particular adoptive practices—differences in regulations, ceremonies, lines of inclusion and exclusion—no single description adequately encompasses Oceanic adoption. Ward Goodenough, contemplating that complexity in the volume's epilogue, asks the right question, one that I am asking throughout this book: "But what is parenthood?"

Despite its utility, the integrity of Carroll's book is cankered by its prejudice. In the first sentence of his introduction, he points out that

DOI: 10.1057/9781137333919

terms like "family" and "marriage" can carry cultural baggage that obscures understanding. Or, in his more polysyllabic formulation, "An important part of the recent development of anthropological theory in English-speaking countries has been the continuing effort to use ordinary English words in ethnographic description without allowing the cultural connotations of these words to distort the analysis that makes use of them."

This sounds like good advice for any ethnographer. Imagine my surprise when, a page later, Carroll offers this comment on the term "adoption": "For those of us brought up in the United States—and here I am relying exclusively on myself as an informant—'adoption' calls to mind the picture of a couple, who have tried unsuccessfully for many years to have children of their own, who finally, with considerable misgivings, have secured a child of unknown parentage from an institutional intermediary, called an 'adoption agency.' "[109]

How disappointing. I assume that, like most of his anthropological colleagues, Carroll was a man who wouldn't dare to publish fifteen words about the cultural practices of other places until he had spent years or decades immersed in careful observation. But American adoptive families can be dismissed in a flippant caricature.

Notes

1   Marianne L. Riedman, "The Evolution of Alloparental Care and Adoption in Mammals and Birds," in *Quarterly Review of Biology*, vol. 57, no. 4 (December, 1982), pp. 405–435.

2   C. Daniel Batson, *Altruism in Humans* (New York: Oxford University Press, 2011), p. 51.

3   William J. Hamilton III, Curt Busse, and Kenneth S. Smith, "Adoption of Infant Orphan Chacma Baboons," *Animal Behaviour*, vol. 30 (1982), pp. 29–34. C. M. Berman, "The Social Development of an Orphaned Rhesus Infant on Cayo Santiago: Male Care, Foster Mother-Orphan Interaction and Peer Interaction," *American Journal of Primatology*, vol. 3 (1982), pp. 131–141.

4   Emily E. Wroblewski, "An Unusual Incident of Adoption in a Wild Chimpanzee (Pan troglodytes) Population in Gombe National Park," *American Journal of Primatology*, vol. 70, no. 10 (October, 2008), pp. 995–998. Romina Pave, Martin M. Kowalewski, and Gabriel E. Zunino, "Adoption of An Orphan Infant in Wild Black and Gold Howler Monkeys (Alouatta caraya)," *Mastozoologia Neotropical*, vol. 17, no. 1 (2010), pp. 171–174.

DOI: 10.1057/9781137333919

5 Christophe Boesch, Camille Bole, Nadin Eckhardt, and Hedwige Boesch, "Altruism in Forest Chimpanzees: The Case of Adoption," PLOS ONE (January 27, 2010), 0.1371/journal.pone.0008901

6 There are many legends that tell of animals adopting humans, none of them supported by evidence. In modern literature, the two most familiar such tales are Mowgli's adoption by Mother Wolf in Kipling's *The Jungle Book*, and Tarzan's adoption by a grieving ape mother named Kala, who has lost her own child in a battle among the apes.

7 G. R. Driver and John C. Miles, trans. and eds, *The Assyrian Laws* (Oxford: The Clarendon Press, 1935), p. 249.

8 Bella Vivante, *Women's Roles in Ancient Civilizations: A Reference Guide* (Westport, CT: Greenwood Press, 1999), p. 94. According to Vivante, an unmarried woman could adopt a daughter, though not a son. The daughter was not a slave, but the mother could direct her either to marry or to work as a prostitute.

9 G. R. Driver and John C. Miles, trans. and eds, *The Babylonian Laws* (Oxford: The Clarendon Press, 1955), p. 75. In a note, "adoption" is translated as "literally: 'for sonship.'"

10 Elizabeth C. Stone and David I. Owen, *Adoption in Old Babylonian Nippur and the Archive of Mannum-mesu-lissur* (Winona Lake, IN: Eisenbrauns, 1991), p. 33. See also Peter Raymond Obermark, *Adoption in the Old Babylonian Period* (Ann Arbor, MI: U.M.I., 1992).

11 Jack M. Sasson, ed., *Civilizations of the Ancient Near East*, volume II (New York: Charles Scribner's Sons, 1995), p. 943.

12 John Sietze Bergsma, *The Jubilee from Leviticus to Qumran: a History of Interpretation* (Leiden: Koninklijke Brill, 2007), p. 34.

13 Alan H. Gardiner, "Extraordinary Adoption," *Journal of Egyptian Archaeology*, vol. 26 (February 1941), pp. 23–29. In a comment published almost two decades later, Jacob J. Rabinowitz argued that this adoption papyrus was also a document of manumission, i.e., the adoption conferred the status of free person on the adopted women. Jacob J. Rabinowitz, "Semitic Elements in the Egyptian Adoption Papyrus Published by Gardiner," *Journal of Near Eastern Studies*, vol. 17, no. 2 (April 1958), pp. 145–146.

14 Von Wolfgang Helck and Eberhard Otto, eds, *Lexikon der Agyptologie* (Wiesbaden: O. Harrassowitz, 1975), p. 36. Unfortunately, the more recent *Oxford Encyclopedia of Ancient Egypt* (2001) does not include a discussion of adoption.

15 Gay Robins, *Women in Ancient Egypt* (Cambridge, MA: Harvard University Press, 1993), p. 77. Apparently, this case was not unusual. According to another source, "Several childless officials at Dayr al-Madina adopted young men to inherit their offices and to carry out funerary rites," Jack M. Sasson, ed., *Civilizations of the Ancient Near East*, volume I, p. 374.

DOI: 10.1057/9781137333919

16   Quoted in Gay Robins, *Women in Ancient Egypt*, pp. 77–78.

17   Joyce Tyldesley, *Daughters of Isis: Women of Ancient Egypt* (London: Penguin Books, 1995), p. 44.

18   Joyce Tyldesley, *Daughters of Isis*, p. 205.

19   Jeffrey Howard Tigay, "Adoption," in *Encyclopedia Judaica*, 2nd edn, volume 1 (Detroit: Macmillan Reference USA, 2007), p. 415.

20   Alfred L. Kroeber, "Totem and Taboo in Retrospect," *American Journal of Sociology*, vol. 55 (1939), p. 446.

21   Claude Levi-Strauss, *The Elementary Structures of Kinship* (London: Eyre and Spottiswoode, 1969), p. 41. Ancient Egypt, of course, presents a notable exception to this generalization. Marriages between brothers and sisters were a custom regularly practiced by Egyptian pharaohs. In addition, scholars have discovered marriages between half-brothers and half-sisters in classical Greece.

22   Kristin Elizabeth Gager, *Blood Ties and Fictive Ties: Adoption and Family Life in Early Modern France* (Princeton, NJ: Princeton University Press, 1996), p. 5.

23   Bernard Knox, *The Heroic Temper: Studies in Sophoclean Tragedy* (Berkeley, CA: University of California Press, 1964), p. 5.

24   These quotations are taken from Mark Golden, *Children and Childhood in Classical Athens* (Baltimore, MD: The Johns Hopkins University Press, 1990), pp. 142, 143.

25   W. K. Lacey, *The Family in Classical Greece* (London: Thames and Hudson, 1968), pp. 125, 145.

26   Cited in Barry S. Strauss, *Fathers and Sons in Athens: Ideology and Society in the Era of the Peloponnesian War* (London: Routledge, 1993), p. 51.

27   Sarah B. Pomeroy, *Families in Classical and Hellenistic Greece: Representations and Realities* (Oxford: The Clarendon Press, 1997), pp. 34, 122.

28   Lene Rubinstein, *Adoption in IV. Century Athens* (University of Copenhagen, 1993), pp. 2–3.

29   Sarah B. Pomeroy, *Families in Classical and Hellenistic Greece*, p. 34.

30   Emma Dench, *Romulus' Asylum: Roman Identities from the Age of Alexander to the Age of Hadrian* (Oxford: Oxford University Press, 2005), p. 115. See also Kevin M. McGeough, *The Romans: New Perspectives* (Santa Barbara, CA: ABC CLIO, 2004), p. 137.

31   J. A. Crook, *Law and Life of Rome* (Ithaca, NY: Cornell University Press, 1967), p. 111. For a detailed account of the regulations governing Roman adoption, see Alan Watson, *The Law of Persons in the Later Roman Republic* (Oxford: The Clarendon Press, 1967), pp. 77–101.

32   Beryl Rawson, "Children in the Roman *familia*," in Beryl Rawson, ed., *The Family in Ancient Rome: New Perspectives* (Ithaca, NY: Cornell University Press, 1986), p. 196.

33   John Francis Brosnan, "The Law of Adoption," *Columbia Law Review*, vol. 22, no. 4 (April 1922), p. 332.

DOI: 10.1057/9781137333919

34 Beryl Rawson, "The Roman Family," in Rawson, ed., *The Family in Ancient Rome*, p. 12.

35 Suzanne Dixon, *The Roman Family* (Baltimore, MD: The Johns Hopkins University Press, 1992), p. 112.

36 Florence Dupont, *Daily Life in Ancient Rome*, trans. Christopher Woodall (Oxford: Blackwell, 1992), p. 117.

37 Florence Dupont, *Daily Life*, p. 220. In his essay, "On Anger," Seneca comments rather matter-of-factly that "we snuff out monstrous births and drown children too, if they're born crippled or deformed. It's not anger but reason to segregate the useless from the sound." Lucius Annaeus Seneca, *Anger, Mercy, Revenge*, trans. Robert A. Kaster and Martha Craven Nussbaum (Chicago: University of Chicago Press, 2010), p. 27.

38 In Plato's *Theaetetus*, Socrates describes the similar custom in which Greek newborns were "walked around the hearth" before being accepted into the family. Those not accepted could be exposed. See Cynthia Patterson, "'Not Worth the Rearing': The Causes of Infant Exposure in Ancient Greece," *Transactions of the American Philological Association*, vol. 115 (1985), p. 105.

39 Stefan Weinstock, *Divus Julius* (Oxford: The Clarendon Press, 1971), p. 189.

40 Mireille Cormier, "Divorce and Adoption as Roman Familial Strategies," in Beryl Rawson, ed., *Marriage, Divorce, and Children in Ancient Rome* (Oxford: The Clarendon Press, 1991), p. 74.

41 Nicholas Purcell, "Rome's New Kings (31 BC–AD 476)," in Peter Jones and Keith Sidwell, eds, *The World of Rome: An Introduction to Roman Culture* (Cambridge: Cambridge University Press, 1997), p. 74.

42 The most extensive discussion of Clodius and his adoption can be found in Hugh Lindsay, *Adoption in the Roman World* (Cambridge: Cambridge University Press, 2009), pp. 174–181. For Cicero's speech, see Leo Albert Huard, "The Law of Adoption: Ancient and Modern," *Vanderbilt Law Review*, vol. 9 (1955–56), pp. 746–747.

43 Paul Veyne, "The Roman Empire," in Philippe Ariès and Georges Duby, eds, *A History of Private Life*, I (Cambridge, MA: Belknap Press, 1987), p. 17.

44 Jerome Wilgaux, "Consubstantiality, Incest, and Kinship in Ancient Greece," in Beryl Rawson, ed., *A Companion to Families in the Greek and Roman Worlds* (Malden, MA: Wiley-Blackwell, 2011), p. 218.

45 For discussion of adoption in early Japan, see in particular, Jeffrey P. Mans, *Lordship and Inheritance in Early Medieval Japan* (Stanford, CA: Stanford University Press, 1989), and Akira Hayami, "The Myth of Primogeniture and Impartible Inheritance in Tokugawa Japan," *Journal of Family History* (Spring, 1983), pp. 3–29.

46 Myron L. Cohen, *Kinship, Contract, Community and State: Anthropological Perspectives on China* (Stanford, CA: Stanford University Press, 2005), p. 116.

DOI: 10.1057/9781137333919

47 Ann Waltner, *Getting an Heir: Adoption and the Construction of Kinship in Late Imperial China* (Honolulu: University of Hawaii Press, 1990), pp. 24, 25.

48 Ann Waltner, *Getting an Heir*, p. 47.

49 Arthur P. Wolf and Chieh-shan Huang, *Marriage and Adoption in China, 1845–1945* (Stanford University Press, 1980), p. 112.

50 Patricia Buckley Ebrey, "The Early Stages in the Development of Descent Group Organization," in Ebrey and James L. Watson, eds, *Kinship Organization in Late Imperial China, 1000–1940* (Berkeley, CA: University of California Press, 1986), p. 18.

51 Myron L. Cohen, *Kinship, Contract, Community and State*, p. 283.

52 The most extensive analysis of this complicated sequence of events can be found in Carney T. Fisher, *The Chosen One: Succession and Adoption in the Court of Ming Zhizong* (London: Allen & Unwin, 1990).

53 Julius Jolly, *Hindu Law and Custom*, trans. Batakrishna Ghosh (Varanasi: Bhartiya Publishing House, 1975), p. 156.

54 Pandurang V. Kane, *History of Dharmasastra*, Vol. III (Poona: Bhandarkar Oriental Research Institute, 1946), p. 662.

55 John D. Mayne, *Treatise on Hindu Law and Usage*, 11th edn, N. Chandrasekhara Aiyar, ed. (Madras: Higginbotham's, 1950), p. 185. The chapter on adoption, from which subsequent citations are taken, will be found on pp. 181–281.

56 Nearly a century after Mayne published his compendium, L. Sternbach noted that "Adoption is widely practised and recognized in Hindu law. The objects of adoption are to secure spiritual benefits to the adopter and his ancestors, and to secure an heir and perpetuate the adopter's name." Sternbach, *Juridical Studies in Ancient Indian Law*, Part I (Delhi: Motilal Banarsidass), p. 541.

57 John D. Mayne, *Treatise on Hindu Law and Usage*, p. 228.

58 James J. O'Donnell, *The Ruin of the Roman Empire: A New History* (New York: Ecco, 2008), p. 173.

59 Timothy S. Miller, *The Orphans of Byzantium: Child Welfare in the Christian Empire* (Washington, DC: Catholic University of America Press, 2003), p. 165.

60 R. J. Macrides, "Kinship by Arrangement: the Case of Adoption," *Dumbarton Oaks Papers* (Washington, DC, 1990), p. 110.

61 Évelyne Patlagean, "Byzantium in the Tenth and Eleventh Centuries," in Philippe Ariès and Georges Duby, eds, *A History of Private Life*, I (Cambridge, MA: Belknap Press, 1987), pp. 610–611.

62 Évelynne Patlagean, "Families and Kinship in Byzantium," in André Burguière, et. al., eds., *A History of the Family*, Volume One: *Distant Worlds, Ancient Worlds* (Cambridge, MA: The Belknap Press of Harvard University Press, 1996), p. 470.

63 Jack Goody, *The Development of the Family and Marriage in Europe* (Cambridge: Cambridge University Press, 1983), p. 72. Although Goody's

DOI: 10.1057/9781137333919

analysis has received a good deal of scrutiny, from Georges Duby, Natalie Zemon Davis, and R. A. Houlbrooke, among other major figures, the general shape of his conclusions has been widely accepted.

64 Jack Goody, *The Development of the Family*, p. 73, with references to Fritz Schultz, *Classical Roman Law* (1951), and P. D. King, *Law and Society in the Visigothic Kingdom* (1972).

65 Justinian also criminalized the practice of infant abandonment. While this would in theory have created a larger pool of surplus children, the decree was probably not rigorously enforced. See A. Cameron, "The Exposure of Children and Greek Ethics," *Classical Review*, vol. 46, no. 3 (July, 1932), p. 105.

66 The Church also mobilized its authority to prevent concubinage, divorce, wet-nursing, cousin marriage, and the re-marriage of widows.

67 Jack Goody, *Development of the Family*, p. 100.

68 G. Robina Quale, *Families in Context: A World History of Population* (Westport, CT: Greenwood Press, 1992), p. 83.

69 The single reference cites a medieval case in which a child claimed as a daughter by Thomas of Saleby was "treated as" legitimate "even though it was notorious and demonstrable that she was neither his daughter nor his wife's daughter." Pollock and Maitland comment: "our law in such a case went far towards permitting something that was very like adoption." Frederick Pollock and Frederic William Maitland, *History of English Law*, volume II (Cambridge: Cambridge University Press, 1895), p. 396.

70 Leo Albert Huard, "The Law of Adoption," pp. 745–746.

71 C. M. A. McCauliff, "The First English Adoption Law and Its American Precursors," *Seton Hall Law Review* 16 (Summer/Fall 1986), p. 660.

72 Cited in Frederick Pollock and Frederic William Maitland, *The History of English Law*, volume II, p. 251.

73 Thomas More, *Utopia, a Revised Translation, Backgrounds, Criticism*, George M. Logan, ed. (New York: W. W. Norton, 2011), p. 99.

74 Edmund Blair Bolles, *The Penguin Adoption Handbook* (New York: Penguin Books, 1984), p. 23.

75 Stephen B. Presser, "The Historical Background of the American Law of Adoption," *Journal of Family Law*, vol. 11 (1971), p. 453.

76 Kristin Elizabeth Gager, *Blood Ties and Fictive Ties*, pp. 44–45.

77 Cited in Betsy Rodgers, *Georgian Chronicle: Mrs. Barbauld and Her Family* (London: Methuen, 1958), p. 68.

78 W. V. Harris, "Child-Exposure in the Roman Empire," *Journal of Roman Studies*, vol. 84 (1994), pp. 1, 22. Infanticide appears to have been tragically common throughout the ancient world. Aside from the practices of Greece and Rome, see for example L. Sternbach, "Infanticide and Exposure of New-born Children in Ancient India," in L. Sternbach, *Juridical Studies in Ancient Indian Law*, Part I, pp. 501–507. For a useful

DOI: 10.1057/9781137333919

survey, see William Langer, "Infanticide: A Historical Survey" and "Further Notes on the History of Infanticide," *History of Childhood Quarterly*, vol. 1, no. 3 and vol. 2, no. 1 (1974). Additional sources include Lloyd DeMause, "The Evolution of Childhood," in DeMause, ed., *The History of Childhood* (New York: Psychohistory Press, 1974), pp. 25–32, and Mildred Dickeman, "Demographic Consequences of Infanticide in Man," *Annual Review of Ecology and Systematics*, vol. 6 (1975), pp. 107–137.

79   David I. Kertzer and Marzio Barbagli, eds, *The History of the European Family*, Volume I, *Family Life in Early Modern Times, 1500–1789* (New Haven, CT: Yale University Press, 2001), p. 217.

80   Barbara Kellum, "Infanticide in England in the Later Middle Ages," *History of Childhood Quarterly: The Journal of Psychohistory*, vol. 1, no. 3 (Winter, 1974), pp. 367–388.

81   John Boswell, *The Kindness of Strangers: The Abandonment of Children in Western Europe from Late Antiquity to the Renaissance* (New York: Pantheon Books, 1988), pp. 16, 46–47.

82   While Boswell's book has enjoyed a generally positive reception, his claims for the survival rate of abandoned children have been treated skeptically by several historians.

83   Philippe Ariès, *Centuries of Childhood: A Social History of Family Life*, Robert Balcick, trans. (New York: Vintage Books, 1962), p. 125.

84   This history reached a milestone in the United Nations Convention of the Rights of the Child, which took effect in 1990 and which has now been ratified by 194 countries (the United States has not signed). The rights of children are set out in fifty-four articles and two optional protocols. The Convention rests on four "core principles": non-discrimination; devotion to the best interests of the child; the right to life, survival and development; and respect for the views of the child. I will discuss another relevant United Nations agreement, The Hague Convention on International Adoption, in Chapter 4.

85   Audra Abbe Diptee, "Imperial Ideas, Colonial Realities: Enslaved Children in Jamaica, 1775–1834," in James Marten, ed., *Children in Colonial America* (New York: New York University Press, 2007), p. 52.

86   Margaret Kornitzer, *Child Adoption in the Modern World* (London: Putnam, 1952), p. 6. "Baby farming," the ghastly and often lethal practice of placing abandoned (sometimes kidnapped) infants with incompetent caretakers, became a particular target of reform. See T. Richard Witmer, "The Purpose of American Adoption Laws," in Helen L. Witmer, Elizabeth Herzog, Eugene A. Weinstein, and Mary E. Sullivan, *Independent Adoptions: A Follow-up Study* (New York: Russell Sage Foundation, 1963), p. 32. I return to this topic in Chapter 3.

DOI: 10.1057/9781137333919

87   Dr. Stanley Smith, Esq., "Adoption of Children in New Zealand, *Journal of Comparative Legislation and International Law*, 3rd series, vol. 3, no. 4 (1921), p. 165.

88   Cliff Picton, "Adoption in Australia," in R. A. C. Hoksbergen, ed., *Adoption in Worldwide Perspective: A Review of Programs, Policies and Legislation in 14 Countries* (Lisse: Swets & Zeitlinger, 1986), pp. 151–152.

89   http://www.adoptionpolicy.org/pdf/eu-italy.pdf

90   http://www.adoptionpolicy.org/pdf/eu-spain

91   Katya Adler, "Spain's Stolen Babies," BBC *This World* (November 20, 2011); http://www.bbc.co.uk/programmes/b016d7hz. The amnesty law enacted after Franco's death in 1975 has been interpreted by the Spanish judiciary as prohibiting criminal charges against those involved in the fifty years of baby trafficking.

92   This story was reported by Ira Glass, on the NPR program, "The American Life," on May 25, 2012; http://www.thisamericanlife.org/radio-archives/episode/465/transcript

93   Ben-Zion (Benno) Schereschewsky, "Later Jewish Law," in *Encyclopedia Judaica*, 2nd edn, Volume 1 (Detroit: Macmillan Reference USA, 2007), p. 417.

94   Cited in Michael Gold, *And Hannah Wept: Infertility, Adoption, and the Jewish Couple* (Philadelphia: Jewish Publication Society, 1988), p. 152.

95   Louis Jacobs, "The Lubavich Movement," in *Encyclopedia Judaica Yearbook, 1975–6* (Jerusalem: Keter Publishing House, 1976), p. 163.

96   Michael Gold, *And Hannah Wept*, p. 154.

97   Catrien Notermans, "Fosterage, Marriage and Kinship in East Cameroon"; and Aud Talle, "Adoption Practices Among the Pastoral Maasi of East Africa"; Edmute Alber, "'The Real Parents Are the Foster Parents': Social Parenthood Among the Baatombu in Northern Benin"; in Fiona Bowie, ed., *Cross-cultural Approaches to Adoption* (London: Routledge, 2004), pp. 48–63, 64–78, 33–47 respectively.

98   See Mark A. Peterson, *Korean Adoption and Inheritance: Case Studies in the Creation of Classic Confucian Society* (Ithaca, NY: Cornell University Press, 1996), and Kuentae Kim and Hyunjoon Park, "Family Succession Through Adoption in the Chosun Dynasty," *History of the Family*, vol. 15, no. 4 (October 29, 2010), pp. 443–452.

99   Everett M. Ressler, Neil Boothby, and Daniel J. Steinbock, eds, *Unaccompanied Children: Care and Protection in Wars, Natural Disasters, and Refugee Movements* (New York: Oxford University Press, 1988), pp. 38–43.

100   G. Robina Quale, *Families in Context*, pp. 361–362.

101   Taimie L. Bryant, "Sons and Lovers: Adoption in Japan," *American Journal of Comparative Law*, vol. 38, no. 2 (Spring, 1990), p. 300.

102   Cynthia Ruble, "Japan's Forgotten Children," *Japan Daily Press* (June 11, 2012).

DOI: 10.1057/9781137333919

103   The data in these paragraphs are taken from Jihong Liu, Ulla Larsen and
        Grace Wyshak, "Factors Affecting Adoption in China, 1950–1987," *Population
        Studies*, vol. 58, no. 1 (2004), pp. 21–36.

104   Junhong Chu, "Prenatal Sex Determination and Sex-selective Abortion in
        Rural Central China," *Population and Development Review*, vol. 27 no. 2 (June,
        2001), pp. 259–281.

105   Lena Edlund, email to the author, November 18, 2011.

106   Arthur P. Wolf and Chieh-shan Huang, *Marriage and Adoption in China*,
        p. 117.

107   E. Chaumont, "Tabann" [adoption], in *Encyclopedia of Islam*, 2nd edn,
        http://proxy.library.upenn.edu:2845/subscriber/uid=1721/entry?result_
        number=1&entry=islam_SIM-8913&search_text=adoption&refine_
        editions=islam_islam&authstatuscode=202

108   Fact Sheet No 51: International Reference Centre for the Rights of Children
        Deprived of their Family.

109   Vern Carroll, "Introduction: What Does Adoption Mean," in Carroll, ed.,
        Adoption in Eastern Oceania (University of Hawaii Press, 1970), pp. 3, 4. In
        1976, Ian Brady edited another anthology of essays on kinship in Oceania,
        Transactions in Kinship, Adoption and Fosterage (Honolulu: University of
        Hawaii Press).

DOI: 10.1057/9781137333919

3
Adoption in America

Conn, Peter. *Adoption: A Brief Social and Cultural History*. New York: Palgrave Macmillan, 2013.
DOI: 10.1057/9781137333919.

▶

In 1851, when Massachusetts enacted a statue defining and regulating adoption, the United States became the first country in the world to recognize and codify the legal practice as we understand it today. The story, of course, goes much further back.

Native American adoption

As in the rest of the world, adoption in America almost certainly had a long pre-history that cannot be fully recovered. The circulation of children, whether through abandonment or informal exchanges between families, must have taken place from the earliest human settlements on the North American continent. The oldest relevant documents produced by Native Americans themselves date to the eighteenth century, but the practices they record probably date back much further.

The most extensive Native American reference to adoption occurs in "The Great Law of Peace," which bound the Six Indian Nations of the Iroquois together.[1] Transmitted orally for centuries, the English translation includes 117 provisions: effectively a constitution codifying the customs and usages under which fifty or so local chiefs (*sachems*) shared governance over an area covering a substantial portion of what would become the eastern United States.[2] Known also as "The Great Binding Law," the document prescribes procedures for the rights and duties of leaders, and rules for decision-making, religious ceremonies, and mourning. Unlike most other legal systems, then or later, lineal descent of the people of the Six Nations ran in the female line. Women were considered "the progenitors of the Nation," and owners of the land (§44).

Articles 66 through 70 deal specifically with adoption. Any member of the Six Nations who wishes to adopt an individual may offer adoption; if that individual accepts, the matter is referred to the leaders, the "Lords of the Nation," for a decision. When the Lords affirm the adoption, they formalize the transfer of tribal identity and "bury" the adopted person's previous clan connections. There is not a word, by the way, about "the order of nature"; apparently the Iroquois didn't share that particular preoccupation with the post-Roman West.

According to Donald Lutz, it "was not unusual for Native-American tribes to adopt newcomers, but for the Iroquois it was a matter of policy."[3] Adoption may have had several motives: to legitimize tribal

DOI: 10.1057/9781137333919

members in the matrilineal line; to provide a home for a displaced clan member; to incorporate a shaman with special expertise into a tribe.[4] Above all, however, adoption apparently provided a way to replace warriors and others who were killed in battle or died of the diseases that de-populated the tribes throughout the seventeenth century.[5] We have first-hand accounts, from the nineteenth and twentieth centuries, which elaborate on this strategy. Among the earliest reports are those of Lewis Henry Morgan, whose study of the Iroquois Confederacy, *League of the Haudenosaunee, or Iroquois* (1851), laid the foundation of American anthropology.

Morgan summarized his findings on Iroquois adoption in his land-mark study, *Ancient Society* (1877).[6] In a discussion of Iroquois social structure, Morgan writes:

> Another distinctive right of the [Iroquois] gens[7] was that of admitting new members by adoption. Captives taken in war were either put to death, or adopted into some gens. Women and children taken prisoners usually experienced clemency in this form. Adoption not only conferred gentile rights, but also the nationality of the tribe. The person adopting a captive placed him or her in the relation of a brother or sister; if a mother adopted, in that of a son or daughter; and ever afterwards treated the person in all respects as through born in that relation.

Morgan claims that death or adoption were generally the two alternative fates for captives, and that slavery was not practiced, at least among the tribes he studied.

According to Morgan, captives who were adopted were "often assigned in the family the places of deceased persons slain in battle, in order to fill up the broken ranks of relatives." Morgan does not make the additional point—he would not have known it in the 1880s—but this "replacement" strategy, as we have seen, closely resembles the rationale for adoptions in numerous Asian and European societies.

More distinctively, a "declining gens might replenish its numbers through adoption, although such instances are rare." Morgan gives as an example (without dating it) an episode in which the Hawk gens of the Senecas were reduced to the point of extinction. "To save the gens a number of persons from the Wolf gens by mutual consent were trans-ferred in a body by adoption to that of the Hawk."

Outsiders, including whites, could also be adopted by Native Americans. Mary Jemison's story is one of many that can be found in our early literature. Jemison was a teenager when she was abducted by a Seneca war party in the 1750s, during the French and Indian War. Soon after joining the tribe, she was given to two sisters who had lost a brother in battle. She described the harrowing ceremony that followed:

> During my adoption, I sat motionless, nearly terrified to death at the appearance and actions of the company, expecting every moment to feel their vengeance, and suffer death on the spot. I was, however, happily disappointed, when at the close of the ceremony the company retired, and my sisters went about employing every means for my consolation and comfort.[8]

Jemison attests that she treated "as a real sister, the same as though I had been born of their mother." Given the name *Dickewamis*, which she learned meant, "a pretty girl, a handsome girl, or a pleasant, good thing," Jemison lived for many years with the tribe that kidnapped her, refusing many opportunities to return.

During the War of 1812, a twenty-year-old Kentucky volunteer named William Atherton was captured by Potowatami Indians, a tribe allied with the British. Marched for miles through mud and rain, Atherton feared that each day would be his last. Instead, once the group reached its base camp, he was welcomed into the tribe. "From what I could learn," he wrote in his memoir, "the Indians had adopted me into their family, in the room of a young man who had fallen in battle." The rigors of life in the wilderness convinced Atherton that "man in a state of nature labored under many and serious disadvantages." He grew to admire the Indians he lived with, but, unlike Mary Jemison, he yearned for release and eventually persuaded his captors to trade him—for a pony.[9]

Lewis Henry Morgan refers to his own adoption by the Hawk gens of the Seneca. This transaction was not uncommon in the nineteenth century, and in the 1840s had even received the approval of the Supreme Court. In *United States v Ragsdale* (1847), an Arkansas district court, after citing the Supreme Court decision *United States v Rogers* of the previous year, concluded:

> The question here arises, whether a white man can become a member of the Cherokee tribe of Indians, and be adopted by them as an individual member of that tribe? [The language in *Rogers*] is too clear to be mis-understood; that in the opinion of the supreme court, a white man may incorporate himself with an Indian tribe, be adopted by it, and become a member of the tribe.

DOI: 10.1057/9781137333919

If Native Americans could adopt whites, whites sometimes adopted Native Americans. One of the most famous episodes was also one of the most unlikely.

Andrew Jackson, an Indian-fighter from his early days, led the campaigns that crushed the Creek Nation during 1812–1814. He routinely broke treaties that were supposed to restrain white incursions on Indian Territory. In his first presidential message to Congress, he proposed the lethal Indian Removals Act, which would lead to the deaths of tens of thousands of Native Americans. While Jackson occasionally expressed sympathy for the suffering that Indians endured at the hands of whites, he more typically called them "wretches" and "barbarians." He may have caused Native Americans more harm than any other single white man in the nineteenth century.

And yet, after the Battle of Tohopeka, which culminated in the execution of more than 800 Creek warriors, Jackson arranged to have at least three young Indians sent to his Nashville plantation, with explicit instructions that they be treated with courtesy. In the particular case of child called Lyncoya, Jackson wrote that he felt an "unusual sympathy" for the boy.[10] Whether he was urged on by a bad conscience or a genuine conviction of benevolence, Jackson explicitly used the word "adoption" to describe the relationship between himself and Lyncoya.

The Colonial and early national period

In the first half of the nineteenth century, the modern meaning of adoption had not yet received definition or codification. Indeed, under the influence of English common law, adoption was technically outside the legal system. Because emergent American law still depended largely upon traditions that "relied heavily upon legitimate bloodlines for purposes of inheritance, adoption was not a legal option."[11]

Throughout the Colonial period, and continuing into the first half-century of national life, the term "adoption" could refer to a relatively diverse set of arrangements. In many cases, children whose parents died or abandoned them would simply be taken in by other families, sometimes kin, sometimes not. Many of these children were treated as servants, excluded from family ceremonies and even from the family dining table. In other cases, however, these boys and girls apparently received

DOI: 10.1057/9781137333919

equivalent affection and care. To give one example, in 1769, a Georgia man named William Russell left instructions in his will that a "dowry of 300 pounds sterling" should be provided to Anna Hunter, "Dr. Joseph Hunter's daughter," whom Russell had raised.[12]

Anna Hunter's life exemplified "placing out," that is the informal transfer of children from one family to another. Typically undocumented (William Russell's will is the exception), this custom was widely practiced throughout the thirteen colonies, as it had been in Europe, and indeed as it still is all over the world.

Apprenticeship was a quite different and more formal system of moving children between families. At least in theory, apprenticeships, then as now, were designed to profit both parties: the employer received the cheap (as in, free) labor of a young person, in exchange for room and board. The master was also expected to teach his apprentice the trade. Thus, in a typical agreement, in 1667:

> Richard Handy...woolcomber, hath covenanted, agreed, and put himselfe an apprentice to and with James Skiffe, Junir...cooper, to live with the said James from 25th of October next ensueing untill that hee judge in himselfe that he hath fully attained the skill and craft of a cooper.[13]

The outcomes of these arrangements, as we might predict, proved to be exceptionally variable. Some young men did learn trades, moved on to independent lives, and looked back on their former masters with gratitude. Others were ill treated, and not a few simply ran away at the first opportunity. Benjamin Franklin, apprenticed to his own older brother, is perhaps the most famous example. Like Franklin, most of these homeless boys migrated to cities; unlike Franklin, many failed to make a new life. Indigent, untrained, and cut off from family connections, many sank into poverty and often crime, joining the roving gangs that terrorized and effectively controlled many city streets.[14]

Apprenticeship often took the form of "binding out," in which the managers of private orphanages were authorized to assign orphan children as apprentices or servants to firms and individuals. This system, which can be traced back to the early 1820s, contained an obvious potential for abuse that was often realized. Children were supposed to have legal redress against cruelty, but justice proved predictably and perpetually elusive.[15]

Placing out was far more common than binding out. In some more prosperous families, children were actually exchanged for longer or

DOI: 10.1057/9781137333919

shorter periods. Several explanations have been offered for the special prominence of this practice in seventeenth-century New England.

Some of these relocations had evident pragmatic motives. For instance, the sons and daughters of re-married widows in seventeenth-century Plymouth were often shifted to new homes. Apparently, the new husbands made the decision to place these children out, not for financial reasons but "as a way to avoid marital disputes and problematic parent-stepchild relationships."[16] This custom was another inheritance brought to America from the Old World: when young Isaac Newton's widowed mother re-married, she and her new husband shipped the boy off to his grandmother.[17]

In many other cases, however, parental reasoning is not so clear. While some historians have seen "placing out" as evidence of Puritan indifference to intimacy, Edmund Morgan suggested the opposite: Puritan parents "did not trust themselves with their own children...they were afraid of spoiling them by too great affection."[18]

The question of parental affection, which has roiled scholars of the family for decades, is part of a larger debate that I reviewed in Chapter 2: did ancient and medieval Western societies have a concept of children and childhood? Did they think of children in anything like the way we do, or was childhood merely a chronological blank between birth and some indeterminate later stage of life? There is no need to rehearse the arguments here. Suffice it to say that probably by the seventeenth and certainly by the eighteenth century, the status of children appears to have changed. From miniature adults, or mere mouths to be fed and bodies to be clothed, children began to assume the favored and even elevated position they enjoy today: "subjects of our primary concern," in Edward Shorter's phrase.[19]

To put it summarily, children were the beneficiaries of what Steven Pinker has called "the humanitarian revolution."[20] The Enlightenment's tangled and much-debated implications included an incontestable advance in the conception of personhood, and the inclusion of children in that conception: nothing less than a revolution.

One consequence of that revolution was the emergence of a child-centered view of children's welfare, including adoption. By the first half of the nineteenth century, American judges were beginning to formulate what became known as "the best interests of the child" doctrine. Emerging initially from custody cases, judges invoking the doctrine included questions of affection and nurture in their decisions. In an 1813

DOI: 10.1057/9781137333919

custody dispute, Chief Justice William Tilghman of Pennsylvania maintained that "our anxiety is principally directed to the children."

Similarly, in 1849 a New York judge explained that when he made decisions involving a child, "its welfare is chiefly, if not exclusively to be had in view. The rights of parental authority are to be regarded no farther than they are consistent with the best good of the child."[21]

The records of a mid-century case in Pennsylvania provide a vivid example of the innovative position that had begun to determine judicial decision-making. A father who had relinquished his daughter to the care of relatives tried to re-claim her after six years. The child objected; the relatives brought suit on her behalf. In his decision, Judge Walter Lowrie found against the father, declaring, "We do not look upon the wife and children as mere servants of the husband and father .... The substantial reality [of the old English common law right] has faded almost to a fiction under the ameliorating influence of American common law."[22]

I hear a patriotic, Emersonian sub-text in Judge Lowrie's rhetoric: the rigor of the Old World's traditional and monarchical understanding of the family must yield to the more democratic conceptions of the New World. In the words of one source, "solidarities achieved on purpose are more powerful—and more quintessentially American—than solidarities ascribed to blood."[23] In short, America, that nursery of reinvention, would re-invent families as well as individuals.

While Judge Lowrie was celebrating America's superior understanding of families in Pennsylvania, Massachusetts Chief Justice Lemuel Shaw was doing the same in his Boston court. Here, too, a father had given his daughter into the care of her grandparents for thirteen years. Denying the father's claim to her return, Shaw decided that the father "had surrendered his rights"; returning his daughter would risk "the happiness and interest of [the] child."[24]

These decisions could look back to a Supreme Court precedent, in a decision announced in 1824. In that case, Justice Joseph Story denied that a father had "any absolute right" to the custody of his child, "but for the benefit of the infant." The governing principle must be in line with "the real, permanent interest of the infant; and if the infant be of sufficient discretion, it will also consult its personal wishes."[25]

In the twenty-first century, this sort of language, subordinating parental (including specifically paternal) rights to the welfare of children, may sound uncontroversial. However, as our earlier survey of adoption around the world makes abundantly clear, this new perspective turned

DOI: 10.1057/9781137333919

the world of domestic relationships upside down. American courts were transforming their understanding of parent–child connections: rejecting the incontestable authority of fathers, and the use of adoption to preserve lineage and property, and embracing instead a vision of family that valued the welfare of children as paramount.

The Massachusetts Statute of 1851

Examples of informal and therefore non-legal adoption can be found throughout colonial history: as we have seen, the term was in use long before the practice was legalized. In 1692, Sir William Phips, the childless governor of Massachusetts, drafted and filed a will in which he left five shillings to his brother James—apparently a scapegrace, "he being heretofore by my means sufficiently provided for"—and the rest of his quite substantial estate to his wife, Lady Mary Phips. The governor further directed that, if his wife should die without a will, the estate should pass in turn "my adopted son, Spencer Phips, alias Bennett, and his heirs." As part of this transaction, young Spencer Bennett, nephew of Lady Mary Phips, agreed to have his name legally changed by an act of the colonial legislature.[26] In other words, while the change of name was enacted by law, the adoption was extra-legal.

Why was the widespread practice of adoption never legalized? Presumably because, as we have seen, English common law prohibited adoption, and colonial charters stipulated that no law could be enacted in America that was contrary to the laws of England. Adoption was finally legalized when national independence, and the growing power of the humanitarian revolution, combined to shape both attitudes and legislation. Thomas Jefferson was among the progenitors of legalized adoption. A vocal opponent of primogeniture, which he regarded as an offense to democratic notions of achievement and advancement, Jefferson persuaded the Virginia House of Delegates to abolish primogeniture in that commonwealth in 1783. Jefferson did not have adoption in mind, but his far-sighted resistance to English notions of blood and heirship helped prepare the ground for legal adoption.[27]

"An Act to Provide for the Adoption of Children," to give the 1851 law its formal title, would prove to be a landmark in the history of children's rights.[28] In place of informal adoption and ad hoc special acts of state legislatures, the Massachusetts statute regularized and codified the

DOI: 10.1057/9781137333919

meaning and standards of adoption. It would serve as a model for other states, many of which quickly passed similar laws, and indeed for other countries as well.[29]

There had been adoption laws in the U.S. before 1851, notably in the South, which had looked to the legal precedents of continental Europe rather than English common law. The state codes of Texas and Louisiana, in particular, took Spanish and French precedent as their models, which in turn created a line of descent reaching back to Roman conceptions of adoption.

The Texas Law of 1850, for example, declared that

> ...any person wishing to adopt another as his or her legal heir, may do so by filing in the office of the Clerk of the County Court in which county he or she may reside, a statement in writing, by him or her signed and duly authenticated or acknowledged, as deeds are required to be, which statement shall recite in substance, that he or she adopts the person named therein as his or her legal heir, and the same shall be admitted to record in said office.[30]

This law, which treated adoption by analogy to the transfer of property, remained in place until 1931.

In many states, prior to 1851, legislatures enacted special laws providing for the adoption of particular children by particular parents: each adoption was the subject of a separate legislative action. "Strange though this practice may seem to us today," one scholar has pointed out, "such enactments were not unusual."[31]

The Massachusetts law replaced private bills and quasi-property transactions with a new conception of adoption.[32] It contained eight sections, specifying the criteria of eligibility and the procedures that would henceforth govern adoption in the Commonwealth. The most significant was the fifth:

> If, upon such petition [by eligible adopters]...the judge of probate shall be satisfied of the identity and relations of the persons, and that the petitioner, or, in case of husband and wife, the petitioners, are of sufficient ability to bring up the child, and furnish suitable nurture and education, having reference to the degree and condition of its parents, and that it is fit and proper that such adoption should take effect, he shall make a decree setting forth the said facts, and ordering that, from and after the date of the decree, such child should be deemed and taken, to all legal intents and purposes, the child of the petitioner or petitioners.[33]

DOI: 10.1057/9781137333919

Emphasizing the requisite fitness of the prospective parents, the Act placed the welfare of children permanently at the center of discussions of adoption, and indeed of childcare generally.[34]

The best-interests doctrine is America's most important contribution to the concept and practice of adoption around the world. Within a few years, the notion began to appear in judicial decisions in England. The Master of the Rolls, ruling in a child custody case in 1865, sixty years before adoption was legalized, declared that the "policy of the law is derived from what is most for the benefit of the child."[35] Over the century and a half that have followed, both national and international adoption codes have affirmed that the leading rationale in adoption cases must be the child's welfare. The long history of this humanitarian insight reached a triumphant conclusion in 1993, when the member states of the United Nations signed the Hague Convention governing inter-country adoption. I will return to this landmark document in Chapter 4. For the moment, note that the decisive requirement in this global treaty is that agencies and governments determine in each case what decisions will be in the best interest of the child.[36]

Orphan trains

The 1850s were busy years in the story of adoption in America. The Massachusetts law of 1851 was quickly followed by one of the most extraordinary adoption experiments in the nation's history. Beginning in 1854, initially under the leadership of a clergyman named Charles Loring Brace, and continuing until the late 1920s, upwards of 250,000 children were sent from Eastern cities to the West and Midwest, where they were adopted (either legally or informally), usually by farming families.

The children travelled on what became known as the orphan trains. The motives that impelled this remarkable episode were naively idealistic; the results were predictably mixed.

The explosive growth of cities in the nineteenth century brought national prosperity but it was accompanied by a sharp rise in poverty and in the numbers of abandoned children. Charles Loring Brace had migrated to New York from Hartford in 1848, with the intention of studying theology. He found a different vocation when he walked through the city's slums and saw childhood suffering on a scale he had never before

DOI: 10.1057/9781137333919

imagined: children begging, shining boots, or selling wilted flowers, penny newspapers, cheap trinkets, and sometimes themselves.

In 1849, New York's chief of police, George Matsell, estimated that over 3,000 children were living on the streets. Children were both victims and potential criminals: girls and boys Matsell called "embryo courtezans and felons."[37] Some, like Horatio Alger's virtuous orphan boys, worked for pennies as bootblacks and newsboys; others survived as pickpockets and petty thieves. In 1852, the city's jails held 4,000 criminals under the age of twenty-one.[38]

The children needed to be defended from the dangers of their exposed homelessness, and society needed to be shielded from the crimes they perpetrated. Many of these young people were the sons and daughters of immigrants, whose influx had propelled the growth of cities in the nineteenth century, and many of whom ended up living in tenement blocks of suffocating density. Poor people had always made up a large portion of America's population, but the crowded slums of the antebellum North were a new phenomenon: concentrated poverty on a scale that was unprecedented. The population of Five Points in lower Manhattan, the city's "blackest and foulest spot," jumped from 300,000 to over 800,000 in the 1850s.[39]

Many of these children spent time in almshouses, which had existed from the first colonial settlements. These places of unsanitary incarceration had always done more harm than good. Often referred to as "poorhouses," they stacked up impoverished families, along with derelicts and the deranged, in filthy locked rooms. Disease and mortality were predictably high. According to one scholar, "thousands of children languished well into the 1920s" in such facilities; "numberless children were conceived in this asylum, and for some it became their permanent home."[40]

Asylums aimed to provide shelter for the homeless and to reform delinquent youth in residential settings.[41] Reverend Samuel Parker, speaking on the third anniversary of the founding of Boston Female Asylum in 1803, asked his listeners to

> [m]ake this Institution a blessing to the community, and the means of relieving the wants, of taking by the hand the female Orphan, whose fathers and whose mothers, by thy providence, have forsaken them, of preserving them from the snares and temptations of a vicious world, of instructing their ignorance, leading them in the paths of virtue and religion, and making them useful members of society.[42]

DOI: 10.1057/9781137333919

Asylum derives from a word meaning "sanctuary," but despite the intentions of their founders, and the compassionate sentiments of men like Samuel Parker, the reality of these places was more typically dreadful. Overcrowded and underfunded, the asylums were staffed by men and women who were often incompetent and were sometimes predatory. Even the best of these institutions offered little in the way of medical care, kindness, or vocational training. Almshouse children were usually denied access to public schools, because of (sadly reasonable) fears that they might spread the contagious diseases, especially cholera or pneumonia, that were commonplace in these institutions. Investigators in South Carolina, reporting in 1857 one of the almshouses they visited as "swarming with vermin."[43]

One student of the asylum movement documented a pattern of imposed conformity, lockstep routines, and severe disciplinary regimes. Shame was deployed as an instrument of control.[44] After all, these were poor children, and for many Americans, then and now, poverty is a badge of dishonor, deserving of contempt. Like their medieval prototypes, American asylums could be seedbeds of disease and nurseries of abuse. Oliver Twist's deprivations could stand as a heightened but plausible emblem for the fate that too often overtook children confined in such precincts on both sides of the Atlantic.

Incorporating the views of officials such as Police Chief Matsell, these "Houses of Refuge" were designed not only to protect children from the streets but also to protect society from vagabond and delinquent children. Even Charles Loring Brace, who regarded the children in his care with more respect and affection than most other reformers, shared in the consensus. Recall that his most famous book bore the unsentimental title, *The Dangerous Classes of New York and Twenty Years' Work Among Them* (1872). The dedication saluted those who had worked to improve the lives of "the outcast and neglected youth of this city, and thus save society from their excesses." New York's "prolétaires," as Brace called them, were fewer in number than those of London, but more dangerous.

> Their crimes have [an] unrestrained and sanguinary character. They rifle a bank, where English thieves pick a pocket; they murder, where European prolétaires cudgel or fight with fists; in a riot, they begin what seems to be about the sacking of a city, where English rioters would merely batter policemen or smash lamps …. [L]et the civilizing influences of American life fail to reach them, and…we should see an explosion from this class which might leave this city in ashes and blood.[45]

DOI: 10.1057/9781137333919

In short, rescuing New York's children would also shield the city's law-abiding majority from apocalyptic destruction.

When Brace founded the Children's Aid Society in 1853, his first projects resembled other efforts in the asylum movement: lodging houses for boys, and then for girls, which offered shelter, food, and rudimentary courses in job training. The brochures he circulated laid out both his rationale and his proposed solution:

> This society has taken its origin in the deeply settled feeling of our citizens, that something must be done to meet the increasing crime and poverty among the destitute children of New York. Its objectives are to help this class, by opening Sunday meetings and industrial schools, and gradually, as a means shall be furnished, by forming lodging houses and reading-rooms for children....[46]

Soon after opening his first houses, however, Brace conceived a radically different way to improve the chances of New York's homeless boys and girls. Having concluded that the farmer's home is "the best of all asylums,"—we hear again an echo of that American embrace of the pastoral—he embarked on a campaign of what he called "emigration." For Brace, the policy brought three connected advantages: farmers would gain additional workers, children would learn useful skills (and good manners) in a "wholesome atmosphere" removed from the crowded slums, and the city would be relieved of the dangers of juvenile criminals. The core insights here, that children will be better off in families than institutions, and that society will thereby best serve its own purposes, remain solidly fixed in social work theory and practice to this day, eight decades after the last orphan train travelled West.

The children varied widely in age, from as young as infants to late teenagers. A typical emigrant was a boy (in more than half the cases) or girl between ten and thirteen years old. They had been chosen by Brace and his associates from the ranks of the homeless thousands, and were told a little about the journey they were about to undertake, though their consent was not asked. They traveled in conditions that ranged from fair to poor, sometimes spending several days in crowded rail cars or Great Lakes steamers that could be bitterly cold in the winter and suffocating in the summer's heat.

The families that took in these children had been recruited by Brace's agents in small towns in upstate New York, Pennsylvania, and across the Midwest. Eventually, children were sent to 45 states. Families who

DOI: 10.1057/9781137333919

applied to take in the children were subject to qualification, including a ministerial letter of reference, but placement was in many cases more casual than rigorous. When the trains arrived, the prospective parents went to the station, or a local nearby gathering place, a church or town hall, where the children were assembled. The children in turn were inspected by these men and women they had never before met, who assessed their potential fitness: how strong were the boys, how polite were the girls, how much did their features differ from the family's norms? Some children had their limbs and teeth examined. The resemblance to an auction is undeniable. In the early days of the program, individual assignments had not been made in advance. Life-determining decisions were made on the spot, in a matter of minutes. Children not selected by any of the prospective families were sent on to the next stop, further west.

From the vantage point of the twenty-first century, the whole procedure seems haphazard and indeed implausible: children sent to places they had probably never heard of, and families taking in boys and girls they had never met. Clara Comstock, who escorted children from 1911 to 1928, confessed herself surprised by what she saw:

> On my first trip with a party of children to West Point, Nebraska, I thought it the most incredible thing imaginable to expect people to take children they had never seen and to give them a home, but we placed them and never failed to accomplish it. The home is always there, it is for the worker to find it.[47]

What kind of home is another question. Given the distance between Brace's New York headquarters and the remote sections of the country to which children were sent, the chances of evaluating the results of this massive project lay between slim and none. In Stephen O'Connor's summary conclusion, Brace and his colleagues were "sustained by a monitoring system that seriously underreported failure and by a prodigious quantity of blind faith...."[48]

Nonetheless, several other Eastern organizations imitated Brace's project. Almost 2,500 babies were dropped off at New York's Foundling Hospital in the two years, October 1869 to November 1871—many of them placed in the famous wicker cradle that stood outside the headquarters on East 12th Street. As it had been in the Middle Ages, such abandonment was in many cases an alternative to infanticide. And 30,000 of those children were eventually sent West on the orphan trains.

DOI: 10.1057/9781137333919

What happened to these tens of thousands of children and adolescents? Some individuals have left a clear trail, whether of achievement or failure; these include two state governors, one Supreme Court justice, several elected officials, along with numerous criminals, among them at least one murderer. The great majority of the quarter-million orphans have simply disappeared from history, like most others who lived unremarkable lives in the nineteenth and early twentieth centuries. We can speculate with some confidence that some flourished while others failed.

The best evidence we have of those ordinary lives is the recollections that some of the children wrote down, or shared with investigators, usually much later, as mature and even elderly adults. Like all such acts of memory, these testimonies are problematic: none of us remembers our past lives with any great accuracy.[49] Furthermore, since the systematic collection of these stories began only in the late twentieth century, most come from the latter years of the orphan trains, when procedures had been made somewhat more regular.

Consulting their memories, some of the men and women who had travelled on the orphan trains recalled acts of kindness. Myrtle Baker remembered that a group of five siblings had been on her train. When they arrived in Nebraska, two of the receiving families "agreed that one family on one side of the road would take three of the children while the family on the other side of the road would take the remaining two. That way they would not be completely separated from each other."

And Helen Perkins Klonowski Koscianski, an orphan train rider in 1916, remembered her adoptive mother's affection:

> Not long after I came to live with the Klonowskis, they were blessed with two more children of their own. More than once, I remember walking with Mama and my siblings. I recall friends coming up to them saying to Mama, "Which one is…" Mama would always reply in a hurried voice, "They're all mine!"

Carmella Schend returned that compliment when she insisted that she never tried to find out about her birth parents "because my REAL parents were Peter and Mary Schend. I am grateful that someone gave me life, but I am equally grateful to have been raised by such loving parents."

Mercedes Slobodny was nine months old when she was placed in the New York Foundling Hospital. Looking back many years later, she

DOI: 10.1057/9781137333919

attested to her "very happy childhood," and thanked the power of prayer for finding the "wonderful adoptive family" with whom she grew up. Mabel Anne Gruele Harrison, who was 98 when she was interviewed in 2007, said that she did not know that she had been adopted until she was in her late twenties. She had been sent by the Foundling Hospital to Colorado, where she was raised by a Catholic couple. Years later, married and working as a speech pathologist, she learned the names of her Jewish birth parents. She called the orphan train movement "a wonderful thing," and added, "I got a good upbringing and landed on two feet. Why should I complain? It was good the Foundling was there to take me."[50]

Other memories were less happy. Lela Newcombe was first sent to Missouri in about 1915, then to another family in Nebraska.

I never knew why I had to leave Missouri, but again I found myself on the Orphan Train, this time headed for Lincoln, Nebraska. I was placed with a woman who turned out to be abusive and controlling. She told me I was a nobody. I was scared stiff of the woman; I was afraid all the time. I'll always remember that day when, in her rage, she picked up my beloved Raggedy Ann doll, hurled it into the fire, and made me watch it burn. I was heartbroken.

Sophia Kral, sent West in 1917, lived until she was twenty-one with a single woman named Anna Greim in rural Minnesota.

All I remember during my entire childhood was working. Anna was very, very strict and I was not allowed much of a social life. I had to listen and perform, as she demanded ....I had nothing to say about my situation. I had no other person to turn to for advice or guidance. I was young and defenseless. I was disciplined to the point of ill treatment.[51]

If Charles Loring Brace emphasized the advantages of his migrant scheme for both children and society, opposition to his movement ran (if I may) on parallel tracks. On the one hand, critics claimed that too many placements were unsupervised, leaving children at risk. A North Carolina delegate to the National Conference of Charities and Correction in Madison, Wisconsin in 1882 charged that children were simply transported to his state and left to fend for themselves. They often ended up as nothing more than underpaid or unpaid farmhands working in cotton fields.

As for the benefits to society, a Wisconsin delegate to the 1882 conference alleged that the orphan trains brought "thieves, liars, and

DOI: 10.1057/9781137333919

vagabonds" into his state, many of whom wound up in reform schools. "I have never seen one that made a good boy," that man asserted, without offering much in the way of evidence.[52]

Of course many good boys, and many good girls as well, found homes at the end of their hard journeys. *Anne of Green Gables*, published by the Canadian Lucy Maud Montgomery in 1908 but hugely popular in the United States as well for over a century, is undoubtedly the most famous literary representation of a child who travelled from orphanage to farm. Anne's trip takes her from Bolingbroke, Nova Scotia, to Prince Edward Island, rather than New York City to Nebraska or Minnesota, but these are mere details. The childless brother and sister who live together at Green Gables have requested a boy and receive a girl by mistake. Feisty, affectionate, and smart, Anne lives through a quiet but emotionally eventful childhood, poised as the novel ends on the cusp of a promising adulthood.

Resistance to the orphan train movement grew steadily through the first decades of the twentieth century. The last orphan trains travelled West in 1929, concluding sixty-six years of activity. Whatever the merits of the arguments over Brace's project, public sentiment had shifted away from placing out to an intensified focus on family maintenance. Today, this singular episode in American social history survives in the Orphan Train Heritage Society, founded in 1986 in Springdale, Arkansas, and the National Orphan Train Complex in Concordia Kansas, which opened in 2007. Both organizations are dedicated to documenting and preserving the stories of the quarter-million children who had taken part in the country's most ambitious experiment in adoption.

From the Civil War to the Depression

In the space of four years, the Civil War created tens of thousands of widows and orphans. The New England Home for Little Wanderers, founded in 1865, was just one of the dozens of institutions established to deal with this unprecedented crisis in American family life.[53] Orphanages grew in both number and size, and adoptions also increased significantly. Predictably, adoption's larger visibility brought both wider acceptance and occasional resistance.

In the 1870s, in one of the earliest book-length studies of adoption, legal scholar William Whitmore shared his misgivings about the practice

DOI: 10.1057/9781137333919

and the new laws that authorized it. To begin with, he complained that "the various statutes on this important subject...have been enacted with very little care or forethought." More importantly:

> In this country, in most of the states, when the relationship of an adopted child has been established, it is irrevocable ....Considering the fact that the subjects of adoption are so largely taken from the waifs of society, foundlings or children whose parents are depraved and worthless; considering also the growing belief that many traits of mind are hereditary and almost irradicable [sic]; it may be questioned whether the great laxity of the American rule is for the public benefit.[54]

Whitmore's crotchety pessimism was not typical of attitudes toward adoption in the second half of the nineteenth century, but his dependence on science—or what he thought of as science—was. Note the appeal to pseudo-Darwinian notions of heredity in his assessment of an abandoned child's life chances. In the years between the Civil War and the Depression, policies in every social domain were marked by a conscious effort to deploy the tools of science in the service of human betterment.

The Progressive years encompassed several decades of reform: in local and national government, health care, elementary and secondary education, penology, and family assistance. The list of innovations in child care reform is quite remarkable:

> Between the 1880s and America's entry into World War I, fascination with the needs of children ignited an explosion that produced juvenile courts, child labor laws, child guidance clinics, babies' health contests, free lunch programs, kindergartens, the playground movement, experiments in progressive education, numerous child study groups, a profusion of organizations (such as the Big Brothers and Big Sisters, the Boy Scouts, Girl Scouts, and Lone Scouts), the formation in 1912 of the United States Children's Bureau, and...new institutions and associations concerned with the special needs of dependent children.[55]

The Children's Bureau was lodged in the Department of Labor and was charged "to investigate and report on all matters pertaining to the welfare of children and child life among all classes of our people." The first director was social reformer Julia Lathrop, who thus became the first woman to lead a federal agency, and who served for ten years, from 1912 to 1921.

These were the decades in which social work was professionalized, and in which procedures were formulated that "remain the basic system of

DOI: 10.1057/9781137333919

regulation of child-raising in place today."[56] Well-intentioned clergy and public-spirited charitable organizations found their authority challenged by men and women with university degrees and state licenses. Indeed, while Jane Addams practiced what she called "scientific charity" at Hull House, the very notion of charity was sometimes dismissed as class-based and class-biased meddling. Critics deployed the cruel caricature of "Lady Bountiful" to ridicule these philanthropic interventions, many of them guided by women.

By the late 1890s, sociology and social work were becoming recognized as legitimate fields of academic study and research.[57] The New York School of Social Philanthropy, the first school of social work, admitted students in 1904. Some educators, most prominently Abraham Flexner, complained in 1915 that social work could not be considered a true profession.[58] Flexner lost the debate. Within two decades the Association of Training Schools for Professional Social Work included more than a dozen university members. In the 1920s, economist Lawrence K. Frank, with funding from the Laura Spelman Rockefeller Memorial Foundation, initiated the discipline of "child science," which aimed to provide a more empirical and reliable account of child development.[59]

The effort to ground children's welfare, including the management of adoption, on more rigorous theory and practice coincided with an emerging recognition of the legal rights of children. While they can be traced back to the best-interests doctrine, children's rights were not officially codified until the twentieth century. The "Children's Charter," drafted by the White House Conference on Child Health and Protection in 1930, explicitly pledged support for an assortment of rights including a safe home, adequate medical care, and a good education.

Throughout the Progressive years, the numbers of orphaned and abandoned children who were adopted remained small. At the same time, in the four-plus decades from 1890 to 1933, the numbers of orphanages rose by more than 100 percent, from just over 564 to 1320.[60] According to a U.S. government survey in 1923, the first attempt to record the numbers of displaced children, just under 65% were located in orphanages.[61]

In short, adoption was viewed as a second-best alternative for displaced children. To quote again from David Schneider, whose survey of American attitudes about kinship I cited in Chapter 1, only biologically created families answered the American search for "a state of almost mystical commonality and identity."[62] In particular, prospective parents

DOI: 10.1057/9781137333919

were not eager to adopt older children, or those with disabilities, or those with records of juvenile criminal activity. For many girls and boys, the main alternative for "children who were of the wrong age or sex, not attractive, or beset with physical or emotional disabilities were orphan asylums."[63]

Fifteen million soldiers and civilians died in the First World War, a death toll that created millions of European orphans and half-orphans (father killed, mother living). By the end of the war, thousands of Americans reached out, benevolently if selectively, offering support to the orphaned children of France and Belgium, while ignoring the children of Germany and Austria-Hungary. Local newspapers were filled with accounts of "adoptions" of French children, though the term was used to describe monthly payments sent overseas—financial assistance that would today be called sponsorship.

Under the headline, "High School Pupils Adopt Orphans," a Missouri paper reported that the "senior, junior and sophomore classes of the Columbia High School have adopted French war orphans. The freshman class will meet next week to vote upon the adoption of one." Several newspapers carried the comments of Mrs. Fritz Kreisler, wife of the violin virtuoso: "My husband is giving up the money he makes out of his public appearances to the upkeep of the needy who have been made penniless by the dreadful war. Out of this, of course, must come our living and sufficient money to support 43 orphans whom I have adopted."[64]

A New York paper printed a photo of ten-year-old Michajlo Jevodovitch, identified in the caption as "the Serbian orphan adopted by Mrs. Edith Bolling Wilson, wife of the President. Mrs. Wilson celebrated her last birthday by sending a check for $73 for a year's support of the crippled youngster." An editorial in South Carolina urged readers to "adopt" French orphans. "Hundreds and thousands of American citizens are 'adopting' a French orphan. By this form of adoption they 'merely' agree to undertake the support of an orphan, the amount necessary to meet this requirement being $36.50 per annum." The quotation marks around "adopting" and "merely" underscore the informal way in which the term adoption was being used.[65]

Adoption in the legal sense also attracted increased attention in the early twentieth century. Some of that history is disheartening. Baby brokers, entrepreneurs with a sharp eye for the main chance, set up shop and eagerly advertised the ease with which a family could be manufactured. "It's cheaper and easier to buy a baby for $100.00 than to have

DOI: 10.1057/9781137333919

one of your own": this was the bouncy come-on in one scurrilous case. At its best, adoption is a humane transaction, but it has also and frequently resembled a greedy scramble. In the decades after 1900, before the practice was adequately regularized and supervised, child adoption "was an exchange governed by an unstable combination of profitability, benevolence, and upward mobility."[66]

I do not want to lapse into sentimentally. Legal, legitimate, and appropriate adoptions typically involve costs, and in that sense there will always be a "market" in this practice. But most of us would regard adoptions based exclusively on a mechanistic, purely market-driven supply and demand model as immoral. Thirty-five years ago, a famous proposal along those lines by two scholars of law and economics provoked nearly universal condemnation.[67]

In fact, this was the situation through much of the nineteenth century. Some children were adopted from "baby farms," unlicensed homes, on both sides of the Atlantic, where families consigned unwanted children for a fee. Typically, inadequate sanitation, bad food, and slapdash medical treatments led to frequent illness and death. One student of these often horrific institutions has determined that the "survival of infants in these homes often depended on sheer chance."[68] Some historians have called baby farms "infanticide-for-hire." In some cases, baby farmers bought insurance policies on babies and then collected when the children died. (Several women engaged in baby farming, most notoriously Margaret Waters and Amelia Dyer, were hanged for murder in England between 1870s and the First World War.)

Adoption procedures improved in the interwar years, as a beneficent bureaucracy made slow but measurable progress against ad hoc wheeling and dealing. Rates of adoption increased in the 1930s, partly as a result of more credible institutional processes, partly in response to an increase in Depression-era homelessness and child abandonment. The number of informal adoptions also appears to have grown. In his 1934 survey of families in the South, Charles Johnson included many stories of poor African-American children taken in by relatives other than their parents.[69]

Government assistance, in the form of a weak New Deal bill authorizing Aid to Dependent Children, provided marginal support for struggling families. However, both adoption and the population of orphanages increased sharply. Nearly 150,000 children were housed in orphanages in the mid-1930s, the highest number on record.[70] Adoption

DOI: 10.1057/9781137333919

became the subject of greater attention to policy makers. One contemporary observer noted that thirty-nine states had enacted new or revised adoption legislation in the decade 1925–1935.[71]

Beginning in the late 1930s the number of children housed in orphanages began to decline. Concurrently, in the decade after 1934, legal adoptions rose threefold, with illegitimate children accounting for nearly 60% of the adoptees. Not surprisingly, unwed mothers were the targets of much moralizing by the moralizing classes. Eleanor Garrigue Gallagher, to give one example from the mid-1930s, was the head of an adoption agency. Her book, *The Adopted Child* (1936), combines useful advice for prospective parents with an effort to defend the (unwed) mothers of the children she placed. It is, she writes, "a fallacy that a girl who has had extra-marital relations is mentally subnormal, or has low morals or ungovernable passions, or a low degree of education...."[72] Such correctives met the strong resistance of received opinion. Women who gave birth outside marriage were typically treated with contempt, which extended to their children as well: the word "illegitimate" was sometimes entered on birth certificates, and the word "bastard" remains a powerful insult.[73]

In an article bearing the sensational title, "Bargain-counter Babies," activist Vera Connolly warned that the "clamor for babies" was luring couples into "a country-wide scramble" for illegitimate children. Marshalling shabby statistical evidence published by the Rockefeller Foundation, Connolly announced that two-thirds of 70 unwed mothers in a Cincinnati study were "pronouncedly feeble-minded." Parents who adopted an unknown infant "have found themselves saddled with a child who is diseased, partly Negro, or perhaps an idiot."[74]

Nasty and racist rhetoric like that reminds us that the dignity of children is always at risk: gradual progress toward recognizing "the best interests of the child" was threatened by the transformation of children (and their unmarried mothers) into exploited commodities. The mercenary motives that corrupted adoption did stir many states into remedial action in the 1940s and 1950s.

The postwar years

Professional oversight of adoption grew more rigorous in the second half of the twentieth century. The number of adoption agencies increased, and the Child Welfare League of America (CWLA) convened the first

DOI: 10.1057/9781137333919

conference on adoption in January 1955—more than a century after the Massachusetts statute that legalized adoption. The conference led to the publication in 1958 of a set of *Standards for Adoptive Service*, now in its fifth edition and still an authoritative guide for practitioners.[75]

The CWLA conference was motivated in part by Congressional inquiries. Commencing in 1953, Senator Estes Kefauver convened hearings of his Subcommittee to Investigate Juvenile Delinquency. While Kefauver claimed to reveal numerous threats to America's moral well-being, in fact publicity was more important to the Senator than serious inquiry: his most sensational attacks were launched against comic books. More usefully, the subcommittee also took hundreds of pages of hair-raising testimony detailing a national black market in babies and children.[76] Although Kefauver introduced a bill to criminalize commercial dealing in children, no meaningful federal legislation followed. (The Kefauver bill was passed five times in the Senate, but rejected five times in the House.)[77] However, tighter controls were installed by most states. The greed that drives many private adoptions will of course never be eradicated, but the systemic corruption of the past no longer poses the sort of threat it once did to the integrity of adoptions.

Adoption has become a fairly routine and well-regulated part of American social and legal life, though the total numbers remain rather small. Since there has never been a single source of information on adoption statistics, "there is currently no straightforward way of determining the total number of adoptions," and the data are therefore conjectural.[78]

From 1945 through 1975, the U.S. government conducted an annual survey of adoption, somewhat primitive in its methodology but generally taken to be informative. The number of adoptions finalized in 1970 was 175,000, the largest in U.S. history. Adoptions then declined to an estimated 125,000 in 1992, which has remained about average for the past twenty years. The lower numbers reflect, among other things, changing societal attitudes about single motherhood. Unmarried women who might once have chosen—whether independently or under coercion—to release babies for adoption now often keep them. For this reason, the average age of children at the time of adoption has gone up, with fewer infants and more older children made available from institutional care.

The census of 2000 was the first to include questions about adoption. Think about that for a moment: a family relationship that has involved hundreds of thousands of Americans, and has roots stretching back thousands of years, waited until the twenty-first century for recognition

DOI: 10.1057/9781137333919

in this country's official self-portrait. To return to the argument I made in Chapter 1, that long delay signals an institutionalized reluctance to admit that adoption produces "real" families. Belated or not, the 2000 census counted 2.1 million adopted children, who comprised about 3% of the American population under 18 years old. Approximately 136,000 children were adopted annually in the United States in 2007 and 2008: a 6-percent increase since 2000 and a 15-percent increase since 1990.[79] A small fraction of these children were adopted internationally, a subject to which I will return in Chapter 4.

While adoptive oversight has been effectively strengthened, the postwar years have witnessed a number of struggles over the meaning of adoption. Let me briefly review three examples, beginning with the debate over whether adoptions ought to be open or closed.[80]

Open versus closed adoption

Should adopted children have access to their birth records, or should those records be sealed? Should birth parents and adoptive children stay in contact with each other? Should the children even know who their birth parents are?[81]

As with all things adoptive, this modern controversy has ancient antecedents. In classical Greece and Rome, as well as in China and India, when the typical adopted person was an adolescent or adult male, chosen to provide an heir, identities on all sides of the transactions were obviously matters of public knowledge. This was also the case in the informal arrangements of colonial America, when children were transferred to other families. On the other hand, in the medieval European world described by John Boswell, which we surveyed in the previous chapter, the circulation of children was usually accomplished anonymously. Children placed on tree branches or on the revolving stone shelves of monastery walls left their natal identities behind.

After adoption was made legal in the mid-nineteenth century, judges, parents, and eventually social workers engaged in a long and often heated debate about the kind and amount of information that should be shared with adoptive and birth parents and children. Through the early twentieth century, adoptions were typically open. Indeed, as late as the 1920s, some women seeking adoptive parents for a child advertised in local newspapers and made their own selections.

DOI: 10.1057/9781137333919

In response, social workers, trying to defend both the integrity of the process and their own emergent roles, led a movement toward confidentiality.[82] They could point to state precedents: in the early 1900s, the state of Minnesota enacted a law requiring both home studies and the confidentiality of records. Other states passed similar legislation, and closed adoptions became fairly standard practice.[83] As part of a closed adoption, original birth certificates were sealed, and were replaced by new documents.

It would be impossible to determine how many children adopted as infants were told they were adopted at all, much less who their birth parents were. Of course older children were certainly always aware that they were adopted, but they might or might not have access to the identities of their birth parents. The logic behind the practice of sealed records was straightforward: adopted children had become members of new families; contact with birth parents would threaten the morale and even the stability of adoptive families. In addition, when birth parents had received legal assurances of confidentiality, unsealing records raised important questions of privacy.

A contrary point of view began to emerge in the 1930s. In a book called *The Chosen Baby*, Valentina Wasson argued that children should be told about their adoptive status. Like most arguments on all sides of every adoption question, Wasson's appealed to the best interest of the child. Where proponents of closed adoption argued for familial stability, Wasson and others favoring open adoption insisted that children would be spared a lifetime of uncertainty if they knew who their birth parents were.[84]

In the postwar years, the movement to open adoptions gathered force. In a book called *The Adopted Break Silence* (1954), Jean Paton gathered the testimony of adoptive men and women to support the idea that adoptees were entitled to at least some information about their birth parentage. "Tell them," Paton insists, "and tell them from the beginning that they are adopted. And tell them something of whence they came and why."[85]

In 1999, the Supreme Court of Tennessee upheld a 1997 statute that gave adult adoptees access to previously sealed records. In the court's opinion, "A birth is simultaneously an intimate occasion and a public event—the government has long kept records of when, where, and by whom babies are born. Such records have myriad purposes, such as furthering the interest of children in knowing the circumstances of their birth."[86]

Practice has followed the law. Though the numbers of closed and open adoptions are impossible to pin down, over the past two decades an

DOI: 10.1057/9781137333919

increasing number of adoption agencies have made the options available. One study concludes: "openness has become common practice in domestic adoptions in this country."[87] Quite a few states have set up mutual consent registries, which attempt to find common ground between the privacy rights of birth mothers and the desire of adult adoptees to learn about their birth information.[88] If there is a consensus on the question of open versus closed adoption, it reaches to a kind of benign (or agnostic) voluntarism: it depends on the individual circumstances of each adoption.

Two other controversies—over matching, and adoption by gay parents—are thematically tied together by a debate over whether the world of adoption should be enlarged: who should be permitted to adopt, who should be eligible for adoption?

Matching

The setting and time: our family dining room, late 1970s. The cast of characters: a dozen or so members of our extended family. Jennifer is about seven years old, and has been part of the family for five years. During a pleasant, noisy dinner, Jennifer mentions to one of her cousins, a boy about her age, that she doesn't remember too much of her life prior to her adoption.

> Cousin: "You're adopted?"

Since Jennifer had been in the family since as far back as her cousin can remember, it never occurred to him to notice the fairly evident difference in her appearance. I am tempted to quote Oscar Hammerstein II's sentimental but compelling lyric from *South Pacific*:

> You've got to be taught to be afraid
>
> Of people whose eyes are oddly made,
>
> And people whose skin is a diff'rent shade,
>
> You've got to be carefully taught.

Some anthropologists have argued that the detection—and suspicion—of difference is embedded in the wiring of our species, a legacy bequeathed by our hard-pressed hunter–gatherer ancestors, whose survival might

DOI: 10.1057/9781137333919

depend on fixing such boundaries. History, ancient and modern, is undoubtedly a trail of tears, a chronicle of persecution and extermination driven by hatred of ethnic, religious, sexual difference. Our human record provides abundant evidence for a malevolent urge that critic Daniel Mendelsohn has called "the impulse to exclude."[89]

But the record is surely more complicated than that. In tandem with our moral failures we have achieved something that one might call progress, what Steven Pinker, in a phrase I quoted earlier, terms "the humanitarian revolution." I would argue that the modern conception of adoption is part of that revolution.

Let me return to the question of altruism, which I introduced in Chapter 2.[90]

Where adoption once seemed to present theoretical problems for a reductive Darwinian understanding of human choices, more recent studies take it for granted: "In a highly interdependent and cooperative species like our own, natural selection may not only have tolerated generalized parental nurturance; there may actually have been a selective advantage to extending the genetically hardwired nurturant impulse beyond one's own offspring."[91]

At the same time, it is undeniably the case that matching on all sorts of dimensions has been a feature of many adoptions, both ancient and modern. Indeed, only in the past couple of decades has the apparent logic of matching yielded to a larger conception of human welfare.

The Greek and Roman men who provided themselves with male heirs through adoption looked first (though not exclusively) to kinfolk. So too did men in China and India. Even today, in the United States and around the world, upwards of half of all legal adoptions involve the familial incorporation of related children (for example, nephews and nieces, or step-children).

Religious matching has also played a large part in adoption, both before and after the legal recognition of the practice. In 1842, the Pennsylvania judge in *Commonwealth v. Armstrong* issued the following ruled in a custody case:

> The patriarchal government [of the family] was established by the Most High, and, with the necessary modifications, it exists at the present day.... 'Honour thy father and thy mother' was the great law proclaimed by the King of Kings.
>
>   The Orphans' Court have by law the right to appoint guardians for orphan children—but so careful have the legislature been of the right of the

DOI: 10.1057/9781137333919

parent to have his offspring brought up in the religious persuasion to which he belongs, that the Court are bound to have respect to this consideration in the selection of guardians, and persons of the same religious faith as the parents must be preferred over all others.[92]

As recently as 1955, a Massachusetts court denied the adoption of twins by a Jewish couple because the children had been born to a Catholic (though the children had not been baptized). The decision relied on a Massachusetts law commanding religious matching, finding—in a spectacular display of biological ignorance—that "the mother's Catholicism is an inborn status dictating adoption by Catholics only."[93] Other states permit religious matching if it meets the "best interests" standard; the New York statute explicitly endorses religious matching.[94]

The commitment to match religion with religion precipitated one of the more confounding episodes in American social history. Linda Gordon has reconstructed the story in detail. Like other nineteenth-century reformers, Catholic clergy had established places of refuge and they had also developed their own version of orphan trains. In the fall of 1904, the Catholic New York Foundling Hospital sent forty homeless Irish children to a couple of small Arizona copper-mining towns for adoptive placement. The New York officials worked with a local Arizona priest to ensure that the children were placed with Catholic families. As a result, these white children were delivered to Mexican families. Outraged white vigilantes, mobilized by the white women in the community, abducted the children and distributed them to local white families—none of them Catholic. The Catholic Church sued for return of the children, and lost. The court decision described the mob actions as "committee meetings."

Race had trumped religion.[95] In the version of the events that Arizona whites told each other—the version that prevailed in the courts—the children were not kidnapped. On the contrary, the boys and girls were the victims in a captivity narrative, and the vigilantes enacted the part of heroic rescuers. Judge William Day, writing for the Arizona Supreme Court, and appealing to "the best interests of the child" doctrine, declared that a Mexican was "by reason of his race, mode of living, habits and education, unfit to have the custody, care and education" of the white children.

Gordon reaches a sobering conclusion, what she calls "a vital generalization about race: that one of the sites most fertile for the bloom of racism seems to be family .... Part of the tenaciousness and adaptability

DOI: 10.1057/9781137333919

of the idea of race is that it harmonizes so well with the emotional secret gardens we construct around family relations."[96]

According to Ellen Herman, in the first half of the twentieth century, matching seemed to promise a familial structure "almost as safe, natural and real as biological kinship." The desire to "normalize" adoption through matching "eventually overtook charity, sentiment, commerce, impulse, accident and other traditional or haphazard family-making paradigms."[97] According to one social worker, speaking for her profession in the 1940s, careful matching will ensure that "no one will ever say" to an adoptive parent, " 'This cannot be your natural child.' "[98]

This preference for sameness accounts for the embarrassment that many adoptive parents felt, and their reluctance in many cases to tell children they were adopted. *The Adopted Break Silence* includes the following exchange, which can stand for many similar family situations. Jean Paton was particularly concerned with the stigma that still rendered adoption a dubious proposition in 1954. She reports that her question, "Is adoption freely discussed" in your family, elicited such answers as this one: " ...No. There is a decided shyness, almost shame, on my parents' part. Even with me they are very hesitant to discuss it. For a long time I felt it was a terrible thing to *have* to be adopted."[99]

Attitudes have changed in the sixty years since that comment, though only to a degree: adoption is still considered second best. In an important 2003 essay, Allen Fisher reports on his survey of several dozen textbooks and readers in the sociology of the family, all published between 1998 and 2001. He concludes that these works showed "little attention" to adoption and "the coverage provided was predominantly negative, stressing the potential problems of adoption about twice as often as its probable successes and rewards."[100]

In one of Bill Cosby's stand-up routines, he recalls how he intimidated his three younger brothers by telling them that they were adopted.

The legitimacy of adoption, in other words, is always under threat. In a sense, matching is a rejection of what adoption is all about: it bespeaks an attempt to deny the distinctive difference between adoptive and natal families by deploying one or another disguise. Resisting precisely the difference on which adoptive families are based, social workers insisted on placing children with families whom they most closely resembled: not merely in physical appearance—blue eyes with blue eyes, if possible, certainly white skin with white—but also, as we have seen, in such invisible markers as religion. Certain countries still adhere to versions

DOI: 10.1057/9781137333919

of these strictures: Colombia, for example, grants preference to prospective parents of Colombian descent; the Philippines requires prospective parents to demonstrate membership in some religious organization.

The implications for inter-ethnic and intercountry adoption are obvious: since such adoptions frequently make matching impossible, they were discouraged, and in some quarters still are—a topic to which I shall return.

Social workers also created a category for children they did not hesitate to call "unadoptable": children of color and foreign children, handicapped and older children, children in sibling groups. It took a generation of leadership, usually exhibited by people outside the professional social work community, among them the novelist–activist Pearl S. Buck, to reform those pernicious notions.

Racial matching—specifically, whether it is appropriate for white parents to adopt African-American children—has presented one of the most serious challenges to postwar American adoption.[101] The opposition to such adoptions was dramatically codified in 1972, when the Black Social Workers of America denounced such adoptions. Taking what it called "a vehement stand against the placement of black children in white homes for any reason," the BSWA statement—recalling the topics I reviewed in Chapter 1—asserted that transracial adoption was "artificial" and "unnatural," and likened the practice to "cultural genocide."[102]

Once again, the long pre-history is instructive, and in this case, the history is heavily laden with irony. For many generations, transracial adoptions were discouraged not by black ideological opposition but by deeply embedded white racism. To put it bluntly, very few white men and women were interested in adopting African-American children. The prospect of such adoptions was so remote that the nation's hundreds of racial laws—which notoriously proscribed interracial marriage—rarely mentioned adoption before about 1950. Two states, Texas in 1907 and Louisiana in 1948, enacted such legislation, but they were exceptions.[103]

A brief, sad story in a 1909 issue of the *New York Times* can serve as an emblem of the prevailing white attitude. I quote it in full:

ADOPTED BABY IS BLACK.
So Mrs. Travers Has Relinquished Foundling Left by Autoists.
HACKENSACK, N.J., Aug. 6.—Two months ago, a new-born babe was found in a shoe box near Peter Wooby's Hotel, Kingsland, and the fact that a big auto containing several women had been seen near where the child was

DOI: 10.1057/9781137333919

found, just a few minutes before its discovery, created much speculation. Mrs. John E. Travers of Rutherford, who felt sorry for the child, adopted it.

Now, however, she is willing to release all interest in the infant, since Dr. Charles Brooks this morning declared that the baby is colored. The Kingsland Poormaster now has charge of the baby.[104]

Few persons, white or black, reading this story a hundred years ago would have been surprised that Mrs. Travers gave up a child she discovered was black. But would any of them paused to wonder what became of that nameless baby, consigned to a New Jersey "Poormaster"?

White attitudes changed in the 1950s and 1960s, and a trickle of transracial adoptions was finalized. The first such adoption took place in Minnesota in 1948, and a slow increase followed over the next two decades.[105] Predictably, the most vigorous resistance to this form of adoption reflected white racist anxiety. Kentucky enacted prohibitive legislation in 1951, and in 1976 (incredibly, 1976 is not a typo) South Carolina made it a crime for "any parent, relative, or other white person in this State, having the control or custody of any white child, by right of guardianship, natural or acquired, or otherwise, to dispose of, give or surrender such white child permanently into the custody, control, maintenance, or support, of a negro."[106] North of the Mason and Dixon line, laws took the form of intimidation rather than prohibition. Between 1952 and 1956, Indiana, Ohio, Oregon, Pennsylvania, and South Dakota passed laws requiring that the race be added to adoption information.[107]

In 1994, the U. S. Congress passed the Multi-ethnic Placement Act (MEPA), which was designed to abolish racial matching in adoption decisions.[108] Galvanized by several high-profile cases in which children had suffered when the best interests of children were subordinated to claims of genetic kinship—what Elizabeth Bartholet has called "the blood bias" in social policy—the Congress was persuaded that "real parenting had more to do with social bonds than with biology."[109] African-American children are over-represented in foster care, not primarily because the system is racially biased, but because the conditions into which these boys and girls are born more frequently include poverty, single motherhood, and maternal substance abuse. According to the authors of a recent study by the respected Chapin Hall Center for Children, "We suspect that many of these children, though not all, are born to mothers who have tested positive for substance abuse."[110]

The law has succeeded in removing a discriminatory barrier and broadening the chances that all children might find adoptive homes.

DOI: 10.1057/9781137333919

The Department of Health and Human Services reports that in the period 2002 to 2009, about 130,000 of the 500,000 children of all races in foster care were waiting for adoption each year.[111] Since MEPA's 1996 revision, adoptions of girls and boys in foster care have increased from about 30,000 to about 50,000 each year. According to data compiled by the National Data Archive for Child Abuse and Neglect at Cornell, transracial adoptions (black children adopted by white parents) have increased from 12% of African-American adoptions in 2000 to 24% in 2010.[112]

In decisions about adoption, abstract appeals to ethnic solidarity must give way when the welfare of individual children is at risk.[113] James McBride, author of *The Color of Water: A Black Man's Tribute to His White Mother* (1996), has said that the white couples he knows who have adopted black children "don't view their children as symbols of cultural oppression but as their children." Children need love, not cultural models: "If a child doesn't get love, education, discipline, religion (your preference) and, most important, a place to call home, all the culture in the world isn't going to make that child a capable, functioning adult."[114] And, in Randall Kennedy's view:

> Racial matching reinforces racialism. It strengthens the baleful notion that race is destiny. It buttresses the notion that people of different racial backgrounds really are different in some moral, unbridgeable, permanent sense. It affirms the notion that race should be a cage to which people are assigned at birth and from which people should not be allowed to wander.

Kennedy argues eloquently that a preoccupation with group identity should yield to a focus on the welfare of individual children:

> Race matching is a destructive practice in *all* its various guises, from moderate to extreme. It ought to be replaced by a system under which children in need of homes may be assigned to the care of foster or adoptive parents as quickly as reasonably possible, regardless of perceived racial differences. Such a policy would greatly benefit vulnerable children. It would also benefit American race relations.[115]

As several scholars have observed, by abolishing racial discrimination in adoption, MEPA extends the achievement of the Supreme Court's decision in *Loving v. Virginia* (1967), which struck down discrimination in marriage.[116] In the words of one adopted Korean woman, "blood is thicker than water, but love can be thicker than blood."[117]

DOI: 10.1057/9781137333919

Ideological demands to re-institute racial and kinship preference in African-American adoptions have continued to find support in sectors of the social work community, despite the inevitable disadvantage that would follow for minority children in foster care, and despite compelling evidence that transracial adoption leads to better outcomes than prolonged foster care.[118]

Gay adoption

This section can be brief. After decades of resistance, an increasing number of adoption agencies are now accepting applications from gay men and lesbians: at least 60%, according to a recent report from the Adoption Institute. (Predictably, many of the agencies in that other 40% are Catholic.) Most states permit adoptions by LGBT individuals and couples, though such rights are constantly under assault by the Roman Catholic Church, right-wing politicians, and other agents of homophobia. According to a UCLA law school study, nearly 22,000 same-sex couples adopted children in 2009, a substantial increase from the 6,500 reported in 2000. Over 32,000 adopted minor children were living with gay couples in 2009, Around 32,571 adopted children were living with gay couples in 2009, compared with 8,300 in 2000.[119]

Acknowledging the parental aspirations and rights of gay people is not merely humane and decent. It is also, given the numbers of American children in need of families, good public policy. Research indicates that gay men and women adopt older children, a traditionally hard-to-place group, and they adopt transracially at a higher rate than the heterosexual pool. A large body of research confirms that children who grow up with gay adoptive parents flourish and fail in about the same proportions as the children of heterosexuals, whether adoptive or natal.

Judith Stacey, a sociology professor at New York University, studied the research and concluded that "there is not a single legitimate scholar out there who argues that growing up with gay parents is somehow bad for children."[120] That finding has been confirmed repeatedly over the past decade. Science is slowly gaining the upper hand against generations and even centuries of demeaning stereotype.

Mainly because of traditional religious influences, intercountry adoption still presents formidable obstacles to prospective adoptive

DOI: 10.1057/9781137333919

parents who are gay. The list of countries that deny gay individuals and couples the right to adopt is distressingly long. In Africa, South Africa is the only country that permits adoption by same-sex couples. Most countries in Central and South America prohibit gay adoption, and the same is true across much of Asia. In contrast, gay adoption is legal in many European countries, with the notable exceptions of Austria and Italy.

Looking back on this chapter and the preceding one, what do we conclude after our survey of adoption's history, both globally and nationally?

All of us would agree that in the best of worlds all families would provide healthy homes for the children born into them. However, we don't live in the best of worlds. As I will explore in more detail in the next chapter, upwards of 10 million children under the age of five die each year, from malnutrition, violence, or disease, most of them in developing countries. In the United States, millions of children live in poverty, and thousands suffer abandonment. For many of these children, the choice is not between adoption and stable natal families. On the contrary, those girls and boys, American and foreign-born, often face years of uncertainty, neglect, and more than occasional abuse.

Notes

1 The original five nations were the Mohawk, Oneida, Onondaga, Cayuga, and Seneca. The Tuscarora joined in 1722.

2 *The Great Law of Peace* is now widely available on the internet. The quotes here are taken from http://www.indigenouspeople.net/iroqcon.htm. According to Bruce Elliott Johansen, the Iroquois "probably have been the subject of more anthropological study per capita than any other group of people on earth." "Preface," to Bruce Elliott Johansen and Barbara Alice Mann, *Encyclopedia of the Haudenosaunee (Iroquois Confederacy)* (Westport, CT: Greenwood Press, 2000), vii. The *Encyclopedia* includes a useful summary of adoption.

3 Donald S. Lutz, "The Iroquois Confederation Constitution: An Analysis," *Publius*, vol. 28, no. 2 (Spring, 1998), p. 118. According to Pauline Turner Strong, "[t]he capture and social transformation of outsiders was a widespread but varied practice in indigenous North America." Pauline Turner Strong, "Transforming Outsiders: Captivity, Adoption, and Slavery Reconsidered," in Philip J. Deloria and Neal Salisbury, eds, *A Companion to American Indian History* (Malden, MA: Blackwell Publishers, 2002), p. 339.

DOI: 10.1057/9781137333919

4   Lori Askeland, "Informal Adoption, Apprentices, and Indentured Children in the Colonial Era and the New Republic, 1605–1850," in Lori Askeland, ed., *Children and Youth in Adoptions, Orphanages, and Foster Care: A Historical Handbook and Guide* (Westport, CT: Greenwood Press, 2006), pp. 5–6.

5   Daniel K. Richter, *The Ordeal of the Longhouse: The Peoples of the Iroquois League in the Era of European Colonization* (Chapel Hill: The University of North Carolina Press, 1992), p. 3.

6   Widely read and influential in the late nineteenth century, *Ancient Society*—along with its author—declined in visibility and authority as the influence of Franz Boas grew. In his essay on Morgan in *American National Biography*, Thomas Trautman points out that both Karl Marx and Friedrich Engels admired *Ancient Society*, as did a number of later Marxist theorists. "The attraction for Marx," Trautman writes, "was that Morgan had shown that bourgeois forms of property and marriage had been preceded by the 'communism in living,' of which the Iroquois longhouse had been an expression." http://proxy.library.upenn.edu:3198/articles/14/14–00423. html?a=1&n=morgan%2C%20lewis&ia=-at&ib=-bib&d=10&ss=0&q=2

7   In anthropology, the term "gens" indicates a tribal sub-group sharing a common descent, usually along the male line.

8   James E. Seaver, ed., *A Narrative of the Life of Mary Jemison, the White Woman of the Genesee*, revised edn (New York: American Scenic and Historic Preservation Society, 1932), p. 39. A statue of Jemison was erected in Letchworth Park, New York, in 1910.

9   William Atherton, *Narrative of the Suffering & Defeat of the North-Western Army under General Winchester* (Frankfort, KY: printed for the author by A. G. Hodges, 1842), pp. 82, 84, 102.

10 Quoted in Dawn Peterson, "Unusual Sympathies: Race, Adoption, and Empire in Andrew Jackson's Household," unpublished essay (2011); this is by far the most searching and comprehensive account of the episode and its possible motives.

11 Mary Ann Mason, *From Father's Property to Children's Rights: The History of Child Custody in the United States* (New York: Columbia University Press, 1994), p. 22.

12 Amanda C. Pustilnik, "Private Ordering, Legal Ordering, and the Getting of Children: A Counterhistory of Adoption Law," *Yale Law & Policy Review*, vol. 20, no. 1 (2002), p. 278

13 Quoted in John Demos, *A Little Commonwealth: Family Life in Plymouth Colony* (New York: Oxford University Press, 1970), p. 70. Unlike apprentices, indentured servants usually served for a fixed period, sometimes as long as a dozen years.

14 David S. Heidler and Jeanne T. Heidler, eds, "Introduction," *Daily Life in the Early American Republic, 1790–1820* (Westport, CT: Greenwood Press, 2004), p. 38.

DOI: 10.1057/9781137333919

15　Stephen B. Presser, "The Historical Background of the American Law of Adoption," *Journal of Family Law*, vol. 11 (1971), p. 473.

16　John J. Navin, "'Decrepit in Their Early Youth': English Childhood in Holland and Plymouth Plantation," in James Marten, ed., *Children in Colonial America* (New York: New York University Press, 2007), p. 135.

17　James Gleick, *Isaac Newton* (New York: Pantheon Books, 2003), pp. 9–10.

18　Edmund Morgan, *The Puritan Family*, 2nd ed. (New York: Harper & Row, 1966), p. 77.

19　Edward Shorter, *The Making of the Modern Family* (London: William Collins, 1976), p. 223.

20　Steven Pinker, *The Better Angels of Our Nature: Why Violence Has Declined* (New York: Viking, 2011).

21　Both decisions are cited in Michael Grossberg, *Governing the Hearth: Law and the Family in Nineteenth-Century America* (Chapel Hill: The University of North Carolina Press, 1985), pp. 239, 210.

22　*Gilkeson v. Gilkeson* (Allegheny County District Court, 1851), cited in Jamil S. Zainaldin, "The Emergence of a Modern American Family Law: Child Custody, Adoption, and the Courts, 1796–1851," *Northwestern University Law Review*, vol. 73, no. 6 (1979), p. 1081.

23　http://darkwing.uoregon.edu/~adoption/topics/adoptionhistbrief.htm. The University of Oregon adoption website is an indispensable resource for anyone interested in this topic.

24　*Pool v. Gott* (Massachusetts Supreme Court, 1851), cited in Jamil S. Zainaldin, "The Emergence of a Modern American Family Law," p. 1082.

25　*U.S. V. Green* (1824), cited in Felix Infausto, "Perspective on Adoption," *Annals of the American Academy of Political and Social Science*, vol. 383 (May, 1969), p. 6.

26　Cited in Joseph Ben-Or, "The Law of Adoption in the United States: Its Massachusetts Origins and the Statute of 1851," *New England Historical and Genealogical Register*, vol. 130 (1976), p. 264.

27　Gary L. McDowell and Sharon L. Noble, *Reason and Republicanism: Thomas Jefferson's Legacy of Liberty* (New York: Rowman & Littlefield Publisher, 1997), pp. 37, 135. Jefferson's commitment to more progressive notions of inheritance did not, it must be confessed, reach to the illegitimate children he fathered on his slave, Sally Hemings.

28　LeRoy Ashby, *Endangered Children: Dependency, Neglect, and Abuse in American History* (New York: Twayne Publishers, 1997), p. 42. Despite its ultimate significance, the 1851 Massachusetts statute "was barely noticed by the press." Christine Adamec, "Introduction: A Brief History of Adoption," in C. Adamec and Laurie C. Miller, eds, *The Encyclopedia of Adoption*, 3rd edn (New York, Facts on File, 2007), p. xxiv.

29　Dana E. Johnson, "Adoption and the Effect on Children's Development," *Early Human Development*, vol. 68 (2002), p. 40.

DOI: 10.1057/9781137333919

30   Cited in Robert H. Bremner, ed., *Children and Youth in America: A Documentary History*, Volume I: 1600–1865 (Cambridge, MA: Harvard University Press, 1970), p. 369.

31   T. Richard Witmer, "The Purpose of American Adoption Laws," in Helen L. Witmer, *Independent Adoptions: A Follow-up Study* (New York: Russell Sage Foundation, 1963), p. 29.

32   By the end of the nineteenth century, virtually every state had passed adoption legislation. Efforts to resolve the variations between and among these laws have led to repeated, failed calls for a national standard.

33   http://darkwing.uoregon.edu/~adoption/archive/MassACA.htm

34   The welfare of the child continued to shape later discussions of adoption. In 1927, for example, after reviewing a number of state proposals for changes in adoption law, one scholar concluded that "all these acts and proposals have one feature in common. They all contemplate an increased measure of state control together with the more effective provision for examining the situation with the child's welfare in view, and consequently a better chance of arriving at a decision in accordance with the needs of the child." Elinor Nims, "Experiments in Adoption Legislation," *Social Service Review*, vol. 1, no. 2 (June 1927), p. 248.

35   *Swift v Swift*, 4 DeG., J. and S. 710, 46 Eng. Rep. 1095, cited in T. Richard Witmer, "The Purpose of American Adoption Laws," p. 25.

36   For a discussion that addresses the best-interests doctrine from both legal and therapeutic viewpoints, see Joseph Goldstein, Albert J. Solnit, Sonja Goldstein, and Anna Freud, *The Best Interests of the Child: The Least Detrimental Alternative* (New York: The Free Press, 1996).

37   http://historymatters.gmu.edu/d/6526/

38   Howard Husock, "Uplifting the 'Dangerous Classes,'" *City Journal* (Winter, 2008), p. 1.

39   Cited in LeRoy Ashby, *Endangered Children*, p. 39. Despite the diverse efforts of humanitarians and reformers, the numbers of "waifs and strays" on big city streets remained shamefully high throughout the nineteenth century. See, among many other sources on the latter years of the century, Jacob Riis, *How the Other Half Lives* (1890).

40   Howard Goldstein, *The Home on Gorham Street and the Voices of Its Children* (Tuscaloosa, AL: The University of Alabama Press, 1996), pp. 28–29.

41   Paul Boyer, *Urban Masses and Moral Order in America, 1820–1920* (Cambridge, MA: Harvard University Press, 1978), p. 94.

42   Samuel Parker, "Charity to Children Enforced in a Discourse," delivered in Trinity Church, Boston, before the subscribers to the Boston Female Asylum, September 23, 1803, pp. 6–7. http://www.lib.muohio.edu/multifacet/record/mu3ugb3481975

DOI: 10.1057/9781137333919

43 Cited in Christine Adamec, "Introduction: A Brief History of Adoption," from C. Adamec and Laurie C. Miller, eds, *The Encyclopedia of Adoption*, 3rd edn (New York: Facts on File, 2007), p. xxvi.
44 David J. Rothman, *The Discovery of the Asylum: Social Order and Disorder in the New Republic* (Boston: Little, Brown, 1971), pp. 225–230.
45 Charles Loring Brace, *The Dangerous Classes of New York and Twenty Years' Work Among Them* (Montclair, NJ: Patterson Smith, 1967 [1872]), pp. 27, 29.
46 The original circular is included in Brace, *The Dangerous Classes*, pp. 90–93.
47 Quoted in Geraldine Youcha, *Minding the Children: Child Care in America from Colonial Times to the Present* (New York: Scribner, 1995), p. 198.
48 Stephen O'Connor, *Orphan Trains: The Story of Charles Loring Brace and the Children He Saved and Failed* (Boston: Houghton Mifflin Company, 2001), p. xvii.
49 A somewhat similar set of questions besets the autobiographical narratives of ex-slaves, collected during the Depression by writers working for the Works Progress Administration (WPA). See especially John Blassingame, *The Slave Community: Plantation Life in the Antebellum South* (New York: Oxford University Press, 1972).
50 Glenn Collins, "Glimpses of Heartache, and Stories of Survival," *New York Times* (September 3, 2007), B1.
51 These stories are taken from Charlotte Endorf and Sarah M. Endorf, *By Train They Came: Fragile Excess Baggage*, Volumes I and II (Denver, CO: Outskirts Press, 2008). See also Martha Nelson Vogt and Christina Vogt, *Searching for Home: Three Families from the Orphan Trains* (Grand Rapids, MI: Triumph Press, 1983).
52 Leslie Wheeler, *The Orphan Trains* (Harrisburg, PA: American History Illustrated, 1983), p. 14.
53 http://www.thehome.org/site/PageServer?pagename=about_history
54 William H. Whitmore, *The Law of Adoption in the United States, and Especially in Massachusetts* (Albany, NY: J. Munsell, 1876), pp. 73–74. Whitmore's book was primarily intended as a commentary on the 1876 revisions to the 1851 Massachusetts statute.
55 LeRoy Ashby, *Saving the Waifs: Reformers and Dependent Children, 1890–1917* (Philadelphia, PA: Temple University Press, 1984), p. 4.
56 Linda Gordon, *Heroes of Their Own Lives* (New York: Penguin, 1988), p. 60.
57 Marilyn Irvin Holt, "Adoption Reform, Orphan Trains, and Child-Saving, 1851–1929," in Lori Askeland, ed., *Children and Youth in Adoption, Orphanages, and Foster Care: A Historical Handbook and Guide* (Westport, CT: Greenwood Press, 2006), p. 23.
58 Abraham Flexner, "Is Social Work a Profession?" a speech to the National Conference on Charities and Correction at http://archive.org/details/cu31924014006617

DOI: 10.1057/9781137333919

59   Joseph M. Hawes, *Children Between the Wars: American Childhood, 1920–1940* (New York: Twayne Publishers, 1997), pp. 72–82.

60   E. Wayne Carp, "Orphanages vs. Adoption: The Triumph of Biological Kinship, 1800–1933)," in Donald T. Critchlow and Charles H. Parker, eds, *With Us Always: A History of Private Charity and Public Welfare* (New York: Rowman & Littlefield Publishers, 1998), p. 125.

61   Susan Tiffin, *In Whose Best Interest? Child Welfare in the Progressive Era* (Westport, CT: Greenwood Press, 1982), p. 105.

62   David Schneider, *American Kinship: A Cultural Account*, 2nd edn (Chicago: University of Chicago Press, 1980), p. 25.

63   Mary Ann Mason, *From Father's Property to Children's Rights*, p. 111.

64   *The Evening Missourian* (January 17, 1919), p. 4; *The Day Book* (November 2, 1915).

65   *New-York Tribune* (June 30, 1920), p. 7; *Edgefield Advertiser* (July 3, 1918), p. 4.

66   Ellen Herman, "The Rationalization of Modern Adoption," *Journal of Social History* (Winter, 2002), p. 339.

67   Elisabeth M. Landes and Richard A. Posner, "The Economics of the Baby Shortage," *Journal of Legal Studies*, vol. 7, no. 2 (1978), pp. 323–348.

68   Susan Tiffin, *In Whose Best Interest?* p. 194. The term "baby farm" originated in Victorian England. See Ruth Ellen Homrighaus, "Baby Farming: The Care of Illegitimate Children in England, 1860–1943" (University of North Carolina dissertation, 2003). Oliver Twist spent his first year in a baby farm. See *The Report from the Select Committee for Infant Life Protection* (House of Commons, March 24, 1908), for numerous horrific examples of children who were abused and sometimes killed in these places.

69   Charles S. Johnson, *Shadow of the Plantation* (Chicago: University of Chicago Press, 1934). The circulation of orphaned or abandoned children among relatives has always comprised a substantial if immeasurable portion of adoption practice.

70   Dianne Creagh, "Science, Social Work, and Bureaucracy: Cautious Developments in Adoption and Foster Care, 1930–1969," in Lori Askeland, *Children and Youth in Adoption, Orphanages, and Foster Care*, p. 33.

71   Carl A. Heisterman, "A Summary of Legislation on Adoption," *Social Service Review*, vol. 9, no. 2 (June 1935), p. 269.

72   Eleanor Garrigue Gallagher, *The Adopted Child* (New York: Reynal & Hitchcock, 1936), p. 160.

73   Christine Adamec, "Introduction," in *The Encyclopedia of Adoption*, p. xxviii. Ann Fessler has collected the stories of women who gave their children up for adoption in the middle decades of the twentieth century. Many of these narratives are poignant, all are powerful, and Fessler has done a great service in gathering and publishing this material. See *The Girls Who Went Away: The Hidden History of Women Who Surrendered*

DOI: 10.1057/9781137333919

Children for Adoption in the Decades Before Roe v. Wade (New York: The Penguin Press, 2006).

74   Vera Connolly, "Bargain-counter Babies," *Pictorial Review* (March, 1937), pp. 17, 95.

75   http://pages.uoregon.edu/adoption/people/cwla.html

76   In the 1960s, the British Parliament also launched an investigation into black market babies. See Diana Dewar, *Orphans of the Living: A Study of Bastardy* (London: Hutchinson, 1968), pp. 83–84.

77   Robert H. Bremner, ed., *Children and Youth in America: A Documentary History*, Volume III: 1933–1973 (Harvard University Press, 1974), p. 760.

78   "How Many Children Were Adopted in 2007 and 2008?" (September, 2011), p. 4. See <http://www.childwelfare.gov/pubs/adopted0708. pdf#Page=4&view=Fit>

79   http://www.childwelfare.gov/pubs/adopted0708.pdf#Page&#x003 D;4&view=Fit A far larger number of Americans have had contact with adoption. A 1997 survey commissioned by the Adoption Institute determined that upwards of 60% of Americans knew at least one person who was either an adoptive child or parent.

80   The terms "open" and "closed" are typically broken down into additional categories: confidential adoptions, in which little or no information is shared; mediated adoptions, in which third parties, chiefly adoption agencies, convey information in both direction; and fully disclosed adoptions, which include both shared information and personal contact. Several authors have emphasized the distinction between "confidential" and "sealed."

81   In the roughly half of all adoptions that involve kin, the issue of closed versus open adoption rarely comes up.

82   The most comprehensive study of this issue remains E. Wayne Carp, *Family Matters: Secrecy and Disclosure in the History of Adoption* (Cambridge, MA: Harvard University Press, 1998). See also Katarina Wegar, *Adoption, Identity, and Kinship: The Debate Over Sealed Birth Records* (New Haven, CT: Yale University Press, 1997). For a recent and level-headed comment on the issue, see Anita L. Allen, "Open Adoption is Not for Everyone," in Sally Haslanger and Charlotte Witt, eds, *Adoption Matters: Philosophical and Feminist Essays* (Ithaca, NY: Cornell University Press, 2005), pp. 47–67.

83   Burton Z. Sokoloff, "Antecedents of American Adoption," in *The Future of Children: Adoption* (The Center for the Future of Children, 1993), p. 24.

84   Deborah H. Siegel, "Open Adoption of Infants: Adoptive Parents' Perceptions of Advantages and Disadvantages," *Social Work*, vol. 38, no. 1 (January, 1993), pp. 15–23. Siegel provides a balanced account of the discussion, but finds "overwhelmingly positive feelings" among adoptive parents about open adoption.

DOI: 10.1057/9781137333919

85   Jean M. Paton, *The Adopted Break Silence: The Experiences and Views of Forty Adults Who Were Once Adopted Children* (Philadelphia: Life History Study Center, 1954), p. 54.

86   *Doe v. Sundquist*, 106 F.3d 702, 65 USLW 2527, 1997 Fed. App. 0051P (6th Cir. (Tenn.) Feb 11, 1997) (NO. 96–6197). The U.S. Supreme Court elected not to hear the Tennessee case.

87   Deborah H. Siegel, Ph.D. and Susan Livingston Smith, LCSW, "Openness in Adoption: From Secrecy and Stigma to Knowledge and Connections" (New York: Evan B. Donaldson Institute, March, 2012), p. 5.

88   http://pages.uoregon.edu/adoption/topics/confidentiality.htm

89   Daniel Mendelsohn, *Waiting for the Barbarians: Essays from the Classics to Pop Culture* (New York: New York Review Books, 2012), p. 65.

90   The literature on altruism continues to grow. Among the most instructive recent accounts I would include Martin A. Nowak, *Supercooperators: Altruism, Evolution, and Why We Need Each Other to Succeed* (New York: Free Press, 2011); Oren Harman, *The Price of Altruism: George Price and the Search for the Origins of Kindness* (New York: W. W. Norton, 2010); and Samuel Bowles and Herbert Gintis, *A Co-operative Species: Human Reciprocity and Its Evolution* (Princeton, NJ: Princeton University Press, 2011). Interestingly and—in my view rather sadly—none of these three books mentions adoption, which is thus excluded from current behavioral research as it has been from histories of the families.

91   C. Daniel Batson, *Altruism in Humans* (New York: Oxford University Press, 2011), p. 51.

92   Robert H. Bremmer, ed., *Children and Youth in America: A Documentary History, Volume I: 1600–1865* (Harvard University Press, 1970), pp. 366–367.

93   Michael Gold, *And Hannah Wept: Infertility, Adoption, and the Jewish Couple* (Philadelphia: Jewish Publication Society, 1988), p. 185.

94   Joanna Grossman and Lawrence M. Friedman, *Inside the Castle: Law and the Family in 20th Century America* (Princeton: Princeton University Press, 2011), p. 314.

95   As several scholars have noted, the court's decision involved a high degree of self-imposed judicial blindness, since at the time Mexicans were officially classified as "white" by the census.

96   Linda Gordon, *The Great Arizona Orphan Abduction* (Cambridge, MA: Harvard University Press, 1999), p. 309. The quote from Judge Day's ruling appears on p. 296.

97   Ellen Herman, "Can Kinship Be Designed and Still Be Normal? the Curious Case of Child Adoption," in Waltraud Ernst, ed., *Histories of the Normal and the Abnormal: Social and Cultural Histories of Norms and Normativity*, p. 205. Anxiety about adoption has not merely troubled American society. Citing Jamila Bargach's *Orphans of Islam: Family, Abandonment, and Secret*

Adoption in Morocco (2002), Herman observes: "... in significant parts of the non-Western world, adoption remained formally proscribed by law and secretive and exceptional in practice even at the end of the twentieth century." "Can kinship be designed and still be normal," p. 207.

98 Cited in Julie Berebitsky, *Like Our Very Own: Adoption and the Changing Culture of Motherhood, 1851–1950* (Lawrence, KS: University Press of Kansas, 2000), p. 129.

99 Jean M. Paton, *The Adopted Break Silence*, p. 55.

100 Allen P. Fisher, "A Critique of the Portrayal of Adoption in College Textbooks and Readers on Families, 1990–2001," *Family Relations*, vol. 52, no. 2 (April, 2003), pp. 154–160.

101 There has been little research on the adoption of Caucasian children by African-Americans or other minority groups, in part because such instances are rare.

102 "Position Statement on Trans-Racial Adoption," in Robert H. Bremner, ed., *Children and Youth in America: A Documentary History, Volume III: 1933–1973* (Cambridge, MA: Harvard University Press, 1974), pp. 777–780. The BSWA re-affirmed the statement in 1977 and again in 1985.

103 Peter Bardaglio, *Reconstructing the Family: Families, Sex, and the Law in the Nineteenth-Century South* (Chapel Hill: University of North Carolina Press, 1995), p. 286, n. 90. Montana required that adoptions be restricted to those of the same race. See Joanna Grossman and Lawrence M. Friedman, *Inside the Castle*, p. 310. Cynthia Callahan overstates the incidence of transracial adoption in the first half of the twentieth century when she claims that "Before World War II, transracial adoption was legally forbidden but very much alive in...unsanctioned practice." Callahan, *Kin of Another Kind: Transracial Adoption in American Literature* (Ann Arbor, MI: University of Michigan Press, 2011), p. 2.

104 *The New York Times* (August 7, 1909), p. 14.

105 http://pages.uoregon.edu/adoption/topics/transracialadoption.htm; in 1961, Minnesota adoption agencies launched a program called "Parents to Adopt Minority Youngsters."

106 http://www.nps.gov/malu/forteachers/jim_crow_laws.htm; SC Code §16–17–460.

107 http://www.jimcrowhistory.org/geography/outside_south.htm

108 The 1994 act, which permitted "some" reference to race in adoption, was amended in 1996 to prohibit *any* use of race in these decisions. Native American children are excluded from the provisions of MEPA.

109 Elizabeth Bartholet, *Nobody's Children: Abuse and Neglect, Foster Drift, and the Adoption Alternative* (Boston: Beacon Press, 1999), pp. 7, 22–23.

110 Fred Wulczyn and Bridgette Lery, "Racial Disparity in Foster Care Admissions," Chapin Hall Center for Children (September, 2007), p. 4.

DOI: 10.1057/9781137333919

111   http://www.acf.hhs.gov/programs/cb/stats_research/afcars/waiting2009.
        pdf. In 1996, following the passage of the revised MEPA, President Bill
        Clinton ordered the Federal government to craft and implement policies
        that would double the number of children being adopted from foster
        care. See Alison Mitchell, "President Tells Government To Promote More
        Adoptions," *New York Times* (December 19, 1996), p. 34.

112   The National Data Archive on Child Abuse and Neglect, AFCARS
        Adoption File.

113   In an appearance before the U.S. Commission on Civil Rights in
        2007, Thomas Atwood referred to a 2004 study in the *Journal of
        Orthopsychiatry* which concluded that "transracial adoption does not
        harm the adjustment, family bonding or normative development of
        children." Atwood, president of the National Council for Adoption,
        also cited *Growing Up Adopted*, a Search Institute survey of 715 adoptive
        families which found that "transracially adopted youth are no more at
        risk in terms of identity, attachment and mental health than are their
        counterparts in same race families." <http://permanent.access.gpo.gov/
        LPS108068/LPS108068/www.usccr.gov/calendar/trnscrpt/092107brief.
        pdf> The data supporting the efficacy of interracial adoption is
        abundant.

114   James McBride, "Adoption Across the Color Line," *New York Times* (June 3,
        1996), A15.

115   Randall Kennedy, *Interracial Intimacies: Sex, Marriage, Identity, and Adoption*
        (New York: Pantheon Books, 2003), p. 402.

116   For a recent and comprehensive summary of the debate, and a robust
        defense of MEPA, see Elizabeth Bartholet, "The Racial Disproportionality
        Movement in Child Welfare: False Facts and Dangerous Directions,"
        Arizona Law Review, vol. 51 (2009), pp. 872–932. The United Kingdom
        took a step backward with the Adoption and Children Act of 2002, which
        authorized racial considerations in adoption.

117   Hollee McGinnis, "Blood Ties and Acts of Love," *New York Times*
        (December 4, 2007) <http://relativechoices.blogs.nytimes.com/2007/12/04/
        blood-ties-and-acts-of-love/>

118   Research suggests that transracial adoption provides equivalently stable
        homes for adopted children when compared to intraracial adoptions.
        In a metastudy, a survey of a dozen studies undertaken in the 1980s and
        1990s, A. R. Silverman found that upwards of 75% of transracially adopted
        preadolescent and younger children adjust well in their adoptive homes.
        That figure compares favorably with other forms of adoption, and with the
        success of children in biologically formed families. See A. R. Silverman,
        "Outcomes of Transracial Adoption," *Future of Children*, vol. 3, no. 1, pp.
        104–118. See also B. Richards, "Whose Identity Problem? The Dynamics of

DOI: 10.1057/9781137333919

Projection in Transracial Adoption," in *The Dynamics of Adoption* (London: Jessica Kingsley Publishers, 2000); and R. J. Simon and H. Altstein, "The Case for Transracial Adoption," *Children and Youth Services Review*, vol. 18, nos 1–2 (1996), pp. 5–22. Perhaps more to the point, given the life chances of abandoned children in any country, and perhaps especially in developing countries, the relevant comparative metric may not be "U.S. birth families."

119 http://williamsinstitute.law.ucla.edu/press/in-the-news/number-of-gay-couples-who-adopt-nearly-tripled-over-last-10-years/

120 Cited in Benedict Carey, "Experts Dispute Bush on Gay-Adoption Issue," *New York Times* (January 29, 2005), A16.

DOI: 10.1057/9781137333919

4
Culture, Nationalism, and Intercountry Adoption

Conn, Peter. *Adoption: A Brief Social and Cultural History*. New York: Palgrave Macmillan, 2013.
DOI: 10.1057/9781137333919.

▶

DOI: 10.1057/9781137333919

Eric Hobsbawm called his history of the twentieth century, "The Age of Extremes," and with reason. The good news: unprecedented progress in science, technology, medicine and public health; extended life spans and a consequent growth in world population from 1.6 billion to 6 billion; the end of colonialism and a growing recognition of human rights, including the rights of women, children, ethnic and religious minorities and gay people.

On the other side of the historical ledger: a "chain of catastrophe"[1] that circled the globe, encompassing two world wars and reaching to countless additional disasters, including China's Cultural Revolution, genocide in Rwanda, Vietnam through decades of anti-colonial warfare, Cambodia under the Khmer Rouge, the mass murder of Muslims in Bosnia, Idi Amin's reign of terror in Uganda, and three generations of Kims inflicting nationwide devastation in North Korea over six decades. The list could be extended.

The unprecedented brutality of the twentieth century does not, of course, mean that individual men and women abruptly declined into novel regions of barbarism. It is rather that circumstances enabled violence on an almost unimaginable scale. Above all, the technology that has brought prosperity and comfort to millions also created the weapons that powered the most sustained and lethal cycle of violence the world has ever seen. Zbigniew Brzezinski has estimated that in the twentieth century over 87,000,000 people, more of them civilians than soldiers, were killed by deliberate human action. Brzezinski describes the politics of the twentieth century, "dominated by the rise of totalitarian movements, as the politics of organized insanity."[2]

Tens of millions of children were included in that toll of death. It is impossible to document or compute the numbers of children who died or were made orphans or homeless in "the most explosive and destructive" century in human history.[3] Instead of numbers, I can only provide a few examples, from the Second World War, the Great Leap Forward, and the AIDS crisis, which will stand for a myriad others.

This is Tony Judt's compilation of reports from just one sector of the Second World War, at just one moment.

> On its route west the Red Army raped and pillaged (the phrase, for once, is brutally apt) in Hungary, Romania, Slovakia and Yugoslavia; but German women suffered by far the worst. Between 150,000 and 200,000 "Russian babies" were born in the Soviet-occupied zone of Germany in 1945–46, and these figures make no allowance for untold numbers of abortions, as a result of which many women died along with their unwanted fetuses. Many of

DOI: 10.1057/9781137333919

the surviving infants joined the growing number of children now orphaned and homeless: the human flotsam of war.

Judt goes on to provide a partial census of orphaned children.

> In Berlin alone, there were some 53,000 lost children by the end of 1945. The Quirinale gardens in Rome became briefly notorious as a gathering place for thousands of Italy's mutilated, disfigured and unclaimed children. In liberated Czechoslovakia there were 49,000 orphaned children; in the Netherlands, 60,000; in Poland it was estimated that there were about 200,000 orphans, in Yugoslavia perhaps 300,000. Few of the younger children were Jewish—such Jewish children as survived the pogroms and exterminations of the war years were mostly adolescent boys. In Buchenwald, 800 children were found alive at the liberation of the camp; in Belsen just 500, some of whom had even survived the death march from Auschwitz.[4]

Since Judt doesn't mention any Asian country, nor the United States, nor Britain and its empire, nor several European countries, one would have to multiply his figures perhaps five-fold even to approximate the number of orphaned and abandoned children fighting for survival on three continents in the war's wreckage.

Less than fifteen years later, Mao Zedong unleashed what appears to have been the greatest single man-made catastrophe in recorded history. The so-called Great Leap Forward was Mao's lunatic attempt to transform China more or less overnight from an impoverished agrarian society into an industrial powerhouse. Farm implements were melted down for ultimately useless metal, harvests failed, and starvation wiped out entire villages. Cannibalism haunted the land. According to Frank Dikötter's recent and authoritative inquiry, upwards of 45,000,000 people died in the four years of 1958 to 1962. As for the children, Dikötter has reconstructed events in several districts.

Child mortality rates skyrocketed.

> In some cases, children were almost the only ones to die. In a small village in Qionghai county, Guandong, forty-seven people, or one in ten, died in the winter of 1958–9: of these, forty-one were infants and children, six were elderly.

That appalling ratio of child death seems to have been typical.

Despite the odds, some children sometimes survived, but those that did faced a grim future.

> There are no reliable statistics on the number of abandoned children, but in a city like Nanjing several thousand were found in a single year. In Wuhan,

DOI: 10.1057/9781137333919

the capital of Hunan, four or five were picked up by the authorities each day by the summer of 1959. In the province as a whole some 21,000 children were placed in state orphanages by the summer of 1961, although many more were never recorded by the authorities.

In short, children who didn't die were made orphans on a scale probably unmatched since the Black Death swept across Asia and Europe in the fourteenth century.

> In Sichuan it was estimated that 0.3 to 0.5 per cent of the rural population were orphans—meaning roughly 180,000 to 200,000 children without parents. Many roamed the villages in ragged groups, unwashed and unkempt, surviving on their wits—which, most of the time, meant theft. Children on their own were easy prey, stripped of their meager belongings—cups, shoes, blankets, clothes—by their guardians or neighbors.[5]

The AIDS crisis has produced an estimated 15 million orphans around the world.[6] Both in absolute terms and proportionally, Africa has been by far the hardest-hit region. According to a 2010 United Nations study, encompassing just nine sub-Saharan countries, Africa is home to over 11 million AIDS orphans.[7]

In a book called *Children of AIDS*, Emma Guest has told the stories of some of these boys and girls, stories by turns inspiriting and heartbreaking: a child-headed household in South Africa, grandmothers caring for grandchildren left behind when parents die of AIDS, cluster fostering in KwaZulu-Natal, young children victimized by sexual predators, countless boys and girls living on the streets of African cities and villages. While she proffers no policy proposals, Guest's portraits comprise an unforgettable gallery of suffering, courage, and resilience.[8]

Beyond Africa, millions of homeless and abandoned children find what care they can in and outside of government and private orphanages. China's Ministry of Civil Affairs reported 573,000 orphans in 2005. In Russia, according to the *New York Times*, 650,000 children live in orphanages.[9] Around the world, 80 million girls and 40 million boys, many of them abandoned, are not enrolled in school. Given the high correlation between education and life chances, these are also sobering figures.

John Berger has suggested that the twentieth century was "the century of people helplessly seeing others, who were close to them, disappear over the horizon."[10] The fate of so many millions of the century's children ratifies the sad truth of Berger's metaphor.

DOI: 10.1057/9781137333919

If I may appropriate and revise a famous statement of W. E. B. Du Bois: the problem of the twentieth century was the problem of abandoned and abused children. And it remains the problem of the twenty-first century as well. Over twenty years ago, A. M. Rosenthal published an op-ed article in the *New York Times* under the title, "Is This Still News?" Here is the first paragraph: "There's no real news in this column except maybe that before tomorrow morning about 40,000 people will die who should have lived quite longer. These people are all less than 5 years old."[11]

Rosenthal's column, which I have had tacked to my office bulletin board since the day it was printed, could have been published yesterday. For more than two decades, the World Health Organization (WHO) and other international aid groups have determined that 10 million children under the age of five die each year, from malnutrition, violence, disease, or some combination of those causes. Over 2 million of those deaths occur in India, another three-quarters of a million in China, many of the rest in Africa and the Middle East. Forty-two countries account for about 90% of the total.[12]

Ten million is hard to comprehend. Nor is it any easier if we break it down: more than 1000 every hour. Every day, the toll of children's lives equals ten times the number who died in the World Trade Towers, and each week matches the total of fatalities in the 2004 Indian Ocean tsunami.

What causes this massive loss of life? The WHO reports that over 1 billion people around the world do not have access to safe water, and almost two-and-a-half billion lack sanitary waste facilities.[13] According to Save the Children, over 200 million children have little or no access to medical care, even the most rudimentary. These are the markers of extreme poverty, which condemns millions of children to death. Six hundred million children live in families that earn less than $1.00 a day.

Children have also been the victims of the hundred or more wars and civil wars and insurrections and revolts and cross-border skirmishes and police actions that have erupted across the planet since 1945: in Korea, Greece, Tunisia, Kenya, Cuba, Laos, Algeria, Vietnam, Democratic Republic of the Congo, Eritrea, Ethiopia, Chad, Namibia, Israel, Jordan, Syria, Cambodia, Nigeria, Pakistan, Cyprus, Angola, Western Sahara, Lebanon, Mozambique, Afghanistan, Iran, Iraq, El Salvador, Sri Lanka, Liberia, Rwanda, Kuwait, Croatia, Bosnia, Serbia, Somalia, Georgia, Tajikistan, Sierra Leone, Burundi, Yemen, Nepal, Albania, East Timor, the Philippines, Côte d'Ivoire, Sudan, Central African Republic, Mali, China, and Libya, to give a partial list.

DOI: 10.1057/9781137333919

Thousands of poor boys (and some smaller number of girls) have been drafted into both government and irregular armies as soldiers. When Ishmael Beah told the story of his experiences as a boy soldier in Africa, he spoke for perhaps 300,000 abandoned or kidnapped children. Just thirteen years old, a refugee fleeing the violence of Sierra Leone's civil war, he was shanghaied by government forces, who turned him into a killer.[14]

A different kind of trap has blighted the lives of child laborers, such as Mark Kwadwo, a six-year-old boy indentured to a fisherman named Kwadwo Takyi in Ghana. Mark worked twelve to fourteen hours a day, received regular beatings, and survived on starvation rations. His parents had leased him to Takyi for $20.00 a year. Mark would not be officially termed an "orphan," since his parents are living, but he has most certainly been abandoned. The journalist who reported this story describes "a vast traffic in children that supports West and Central African fisheries, quarries, cocoa and rice plantations and street markets." Boys labor as boat crew, field hands, and miners. Girls are imprisoned as domestic servants, cooks, and prostitutes.[15]

All international humanitarian intervention—medical assistance, constitution-making, and in-country development—is propelled by the desire to help some of the world's children find the stability and the health and the homes that will enable them to survive, and perhaps even to flourish. Intercountry adoption is a small but necessary instrument in that effort.

Homeless children came to the United States from Europe in small numbers in the first half of the twentieth century. As part of the Displaced Persons Act of 1918, Congress authorized the entry of "displaced orphans." However, the numbers remained small: from 1935 through 1948, only 14 immigrants per year entered the country in the category "under 16 years of age, unaccompanied by parents."[16]

Following the Second World War, intercountry adoption expanded at the intersection of intensified crises, especially widespread poverty and continuing warfare, changing notions of humanitarian intervention, and technologies that have enabled the movement of abandoned children across national boundaries.

One of the leading figures in this humanitarian transformation was Pearl S. Buck. Born in 1892 to missionary parents, Buck had spent most of her first forty years in China. When she returned permanently to the

DOI: 10.1057/9781137333919

United States in the mid-1930s, she commenced a career of social and political activism that she would pursue for four decades, until her death in 1973.

Beginning almost immediately on her return to the U.S., she established herself as a leading voice in the campaign for civil rights, publishing essays demanding African-American equality in the NAACP magazine, *Crisis*, and in the Urban League's journal, *Opportunity*. In 1942, the NAACP executive secretary, Walter White, said that Buck was one of only two white Americans who understood the reality of black life; the other was Eleanor Roosevelt. In her essays and speeches, Buck also championed equal rights for women, whose circumstances in 1930s America she called "medieval." She gave vigorous support to the Equal Rights Amendment, at a time when the majority of women's organizations stood in opposition.

Above all, Buck tried to serve as spokeswoman for the world's impoverished, abandoned, and handicapped children. Her commitment reached deep into her personal life: she adopted seven children, two of them mixed-race, and served as foster mother to several more. She emerged as a leading figure in adoptive practice more or less by chance. Because of her reputation as an advocate for children and people of color, Buck was approached in 1948 by two sets of mixed-race parents who had reluctantly decided to release their infant children for adoption. No American agency would even attempt to place them; mixed-race children were written off as unadoptable.

Buck later recalled her reaction:

> "I called adoption agencies and told them of these two beautiful children. Everywhere I was faced with the same answer, they could not place these children because they could not match parents. I was so indignant I started my own damned agency."[17]

So, in 1949, using as headquarters a house near her home in suburban Philadelphia, Buck founded Welcome House, the world's first interracial, intercountry adoption agency. She recruited friends and neighbors to the board, including Oscar Hammerstein, II, and James Michener. She raised money and consciousness. She lobbied successfully for legislative reform. And she helped to launch a humanitarian revolution.

It has been, to be sure, revolution on a fairly small scale, when measured against the magnitude of the crisis that the world's children face. Accurate numbers for the years before 1971 are hard to pin down, but

DOI: 10.1057/9781137333919

I would estimate that in the sixty-plus years since Welcome House and similar organizations began their work, upwards of 800,000 children have come to the U.S. for adoption.[18] While these adoptions tripled from 6,472 in 1992 to 19,237 in 2001, and peaked at 22,884 in 2004, the numbers have since declined—I am tempted to say collapsed—to 9,319 in 2011. I will comment later on this significant decrease in intercountry adoptions.

Among those who followed in the wake of Pearl Buck's humanitarian pioneer efforts, Harry and Bertha Holt were the most active. The Holts were evangelical Christians, and the organization they founded in 1955, Holt International, continues to describe its mission in religious terms. Pearl Buck was uncomfortable with that sort of rhetoric, but she defended the work that both the Holts and Welcome House did, arguing against the commitment to matching that, as we have seen, still dominated professional social work.

The process through which prospective adoptive parents go is rigorous—rightly so—and the hoops and hurdles are even more challenging in the case of international adoption, since the laws and regulations of two countries must be observed. When Terry and I embarked on our own quest, in the early 1970s, we were scrutinized to a fare-thee-well. We were visited at home several times by a social worker who interviewed us at length and looked through our apartment. We were fingerprinted, and put through a background check. We had to provide all of our financial and medical records. We solicited references from friends and employers. Our three natal children were interviewed, separately and together. We supplied photographs of our apartment, both interior and exterior views.

As we remarked on several occasions, no one ever questioned our competence as potential parents when we simply reproduced. At the same time, we were happy to comply with the assorted investigations, which are intended to protect children from the damage that a bad placement can inflict.

We began to plan for Jennifer's arrival only after our application had been approved both in the U.S. and Korea. In most intercountry adoptions, parents travel to the country to be joined with their new child. Children adopted from Korea, on the other hand, travel to their new country in the company of certified escorts, usually adoption agency personnel. So, on a snowy day in February, 1975, Terry and I and our three children drove to Kennedy Airport to meet Jennifer and bring her home. That event was among the most unforgettable of our lives.

DOI: 10.1057/9781137333919

A dozen or so prospective new parents were gathered in the airport waiting room. When the plane landed, safely and more or less on time, the collective sigh of relief was probably audible fifty yards away. We waited with as much patience as we could while all the regular passengers exited the plane first. Then, after a pause of about two minutes that felt like an hour, escorts began to walk down the ramp holding the babies and young children with whom they had been traveling for the past thirty hours. As each name was called, the families would identify themselves and the escort handed the child to its new parents.

Many years ago, in the "News from Lake Wobegon," Garrison Keillor told us that Darryl and Lucille Tollerud had met their new Korean child at the Minneapolis airport earlier that week. When Keillor got to the point in his story that I have reached in mine—parents and children waiting to meet the young strangers who were about to become permanent members of their families—he said that an extraordinary thing happened. As their anxieties escalated to unprecedented levels, everyone in the waiting room simply left the ground and hovered several inches in the air. I believe Terry and I and our children had the same experience.

An hour later, as we sat with Jennifer in the nearly empty airport lounge, our joy in her safe arrival contended with sadness. We did not know the details of her abandonment, but we knew that her life had already been scarred by tragedy. Adoption almost always finds its origins in the displacements that accompany poverty and war.

In April 1975, shortly after Jennifer's arrival, the American defeat in Vietnam precipitated what was called "Operation Babylift," a mass evacuation of infants and children (mainly) from Saigon. An estimated 3,500 boys and girls were flown for adoption to the U.S., Australia, France, and Canada. The outcomes for most of the children—as is usually the case in intercountry adoptions—have included success and failure in the proportions found in all families, adoptive or not. Because of the conditions under which the operation proceeded, mistakes were made. While the children considered eligible for transport were Vietnamese and mixed-race orphans, a combination of haste and occasional negligence led to the inclusion of a small number of children from intact families in the operation.

Many of the Vietnamese children were brought to America by Welcome House, which also supervised Jennifer's adoption. In the six decades since the agency was founded by Pearl Buck, Welcome House

DOI: 10.1057/9781137333919

has assisted in some 6,500 adoptions; Holt International has been responsible for the adoption of another 40,000 children. Dozens of other agencies have joined them in the past half-century.

Across the entire postwar period, the largest number of children has come to America from South Korea, followed by China, Russia, Guatemala, Ethiopia, Vietnam, Ukraine, Colombia, Kazakhstan, and Romania (the last in direct response to the humanitarian crisis that followed the collapse of dictator Nicolae Ceausescu in 1989). Adopted boys and girls in lesser numbers have also come from dozens of other countries, including Cambodia, Haiti, Pakistan, the Philippines, India, Liberia, Ghana, Bulgaria, Ecuador, Peru, and Bolivia. Somewhat surprisingly, at least to me, more than eighty countries have sent children to the United States in the past several decades: 18 countries in Central and South America, more than 30 in Africa, nearly 40 in the Middle East, Asia, and Oceania.

Along with America, a number of other countries, mainly in Europe, have also provided homes for children adopted across borders. The receiving countries with the highest number of intercountry adoptions in the most recent survey include (in rank order) France, Italy, Canada, Spain, Sweden, Germany, Netherlands, Norway, Denmark, Belgium, Switzerland, Australia, and Finland. Taken together, these destination countries have received slightly more children than the United States. So, adding these non-U.S. adoptions to the American totals, a reasonable estimate of the number of intercountry adoptions between the Second World War and 2010 would be nearly 2 million children. Two million is a large number, though only a fraction of the world's homeless and abandoned children.

Whether on the streets or resident in orphanages, life for abandoned children, especially in developing countries, is excruciatingly hard. In 1996, reports out of China revealed a dreadful pattern of neglect and abuse in state orphanages that provoked international outrage.

These conditions first gained attention in a 1995 British documentary film called "The Dying Rooms." Kate Blewett, one of the producers, used a false identity and a hidden camera to film inside a Guangdong orphanage. Shortly after the film's release, Human Rights Watch published a book-length accusation of Chinese behavior under the title *Death By Default.* The report accused the Chinese government of effectively condemning thousands of orphaned children to death. Mortality rates in Chinese 67 state-run orphanages were far higher than in any

DOI: 10.1057/9781137333919

other country: in the provinces of Fujian, Shaanxi, Guangxi and Henan, mortality ranged from 59.2 percent to 72.5 percent. Some of these deaths followed from colossal negligence while others were deliberate: the institutional killing fields were adequately funded and staffed; local and national authorities were aware of the lethal conditions; the government's reaction to the revelations was denial and cover-up.

Along with documents, statistical analyses, photographs, and tables of data, *Death by Default* includes heartrending stories of individual children. The book details abuse and ill treatment including sexual assault, beatings, and medical negligence. Scores of infants were given so little food that they starved to death. Older children who choked on food were permitted to die. Infants and small children were routinely tied to beds, cribs, and chairs to spare the staff inconvenience. Children were frequently given sedatives to keep them quiet, with fatal consequences. Perceived misbehavior brought punishment that can only be called torture, including a form of water boarding:

> ...hanging children upside down with their heads submerged in water, until nosebleeds and near-suffocation ensued. This technique, known as *qiang shui* ("choking on water"), was reportedly the one most feared by children.[19]

In large part because of China's one-child policy, and also because of the deeply rooted Chinese devaluation of girls and women, 90% of the inmates of China's orphanages are girls. The country has experienced an epidemic of child abandonment: "Babies, female babies, it seemed were found everywhere, every day. Babies in sunlight and babies in moonlight. Babies wrapped in newspapers, babies bundled in rags, babies in baskets, babies in boxes."[20]

This gender imbalance reflects one of the world's most important social realities. While boys and girls share the burdens of poverty and homelessness, girls have also been trapped by cultural and religious traditions that relegate them to a lower order of humanity, less valuable and therefore less entitled to protection. This anti-female bigotry is of course ratified and reinforced by most of the world's religions: Judaism, Islam, Hinduism, Christianity, especially in its Roman Catholic variant, and the quasi-religious tenets of Confucianism. While violent acts against girls and women are sadly common throughout the world, they occur on the most destructive scale in Africa and Asia.

Over twenty years ago, Amartya Sen published an essay with the shocking title, "More Than 100 Million Women Are Missing." Using a

DOI: 10.1057/9781137333919

benchmark ratio of 1.05 women to men—the figure that obtains across the developed world, where boys and girls are reared under more or less equal conditions—and comparing that with the percentage across Asia and Africa, Sen calculated that

> in China alone this amounts to 50 million "missing women." When that number is added to those in South Asia, West Asia, and North Africa, a great many more than 100 million women are "missing." These numbers tell us, quietly, a terrible story of inequality and neglect leading to the excess mortality of women.[21]

What lies behind these horrific numbers? Some explanations appeal to the alleged difference between Western and Eastern "values." However, since Japan has about the same sex ratio as Europe and the United States, that analysis can be no more than partial. Economic underdevelopment obviously plays a role, though in fact several underdeveloped regions, including sub-Saharan Africa, have a surplus rather than a deficit of women. Rather, the fate of the missing women is the result of a complex interaction among poverty, tradition, and government policies.

What Sen called "one of the more momentous, and neglected, problems facing the world today" has not been solved, or even substantially alleviated in the twenty years since his essay appeared. Indeed, the situation seems in many regions to be getting worse, according to a 2004 book called *Bare Branches,* which includes tables enumerating Asia's surplus male population. There are about 110 million more males in China than females, and India has reached equivalent proportions, based on similar patterns of sex-selective abortions, female infanticide, differential nutritional support, and inadequate medical care. Repeating Amartya Sen's earlier comment about missing women, the book's authors conclude that the "masculinization of Asia's sex ratios is one of the overlooked stories of the century."[22]

In March, 2010, the *Economist* published both a leading article and an extended essay under the heading, "The War on Baby Girls." After reviewing the gender imbalances I have just summarized, the editors suggest that "it is no exaggeration to call this gendercide."[23]

Maxine Hong Kingston, reconstructing her Chinese–American childhood, recalled some of the many proverbs she heard when she was growing up, customary sayings that condemned girls for the crime of being female. "Feeding girls is feeding cowbirds...better to raise geese than girls...girls are maggots in the rice."[24]

DOI: 10.1057/9781137333919

Attitudes like this, whether explicit or implicit, sustain such practices as female genital mutilation, which has been inflicted on an estimated 140 million girls and women,[25] child marriages, to which as many as 10 million girls are subjected each year, sex trafficking in girls, "bride burnings," or dowry deaths, which have been occurring in India at the rate of 6,000 each year since the mid-1990s,[26] and female infanticide, reliably reported in Tamil Nadu and other South Asian regions.[27]

These are some of the facts on the ground. In the framework of that grim survey, the significant decrease in intercountry adoptions, which I cited earlier, may seem puzzling. The numbers of homeless, abandoned, and threatened children have not decreased, but the numbers of those children finding homes across borders have in the past few years been reduced by more than half in the U.S. and by similar proportions around the developed world. Why?

I would propose several quite different explanations. To begin with, some of the decline followed quite properly from the increasing self-sufficiency of several developing nations. South Korea, to give a prominent example, has transformed itself economically over the past four or so decades. Following thirty-five years of Japanese occupation, and the ravages of a brutal civil war, Korea until the 1970s was a genuinely poor country. Today Korea's economy is among the ten largest in the world, and it has been moving, more slowly than it should but steadily, toward a commensurate increase in domestic adoption. A similar progression can be observed in China and Thailand.

In addition, a number of scandals and controversies have understandably aroused suspicion about adoption across borders. To put it bluntly, some of the 2 million adoptions that have taken place across borders should have been prevented.

Among the most egregious examples was the corrupt behavior that infected adoption from Vietnam for much of the 2000 decade. Widely reported in 2010, a trail of documents revealed a network of conspirators at every governmental level, including adoption agency representatives, village officials, orphanage directors, nurses, hospital administrators, police officers, and government officials, "who were profiting by paying for, defrauding, coercing, or even simply stealing Vietnamese children from their families to sell them to unsuspecting Americans."[28] A similar pattern of ruthless corruption has undermined the integrity of adoptions from Guatemala.

DOI: 10.1057/9781137333919

Ireland was the scene of a less widely reported scandal, an export business in babies that sent thousands of infants and young children to America in the 1950s and 1960s. These boys and girls, taken from their unmarried mothers by priests and nuns, were declared to be "orphans" and were sold to American parents whose suitability had never been investigated. For a generation, the Irish government simply delegated its welfare regime to the Catholic Church, with disastrous results for untold children.[29]

Those of us who want to bear witness to the efficacy and legitimacy of intercountry adoption can only feel shame and anger about the inhumanity of these black markets in babies. At the same time, I think we can assert with some confidence that such episodes are exceptions. If not, there would have been more stories than there have been. To return to A. M. Rosenthal's 1996 *New York Times* article, it is not news that 30,000 children die each day; however, corruption in intercountry adoption is always news.

Bear in mind that many of those children die at the hands of their birth parents. Exemplifying the murderous violence with which natal children are sometimes threatened, consider a photograph published recently in the *New York Times*, which pictured a weeping mother holding her dead infant daughter. The caption, in its entirety: "Reshma Bano holding the body of her 3-month-old daughter, Neha Afreen, on Wednesday outside a hospital morgue in Bangalore, India. The police say the child's father beat her for being born a girl, a violent reflection of India's cultural preference for sons."[30]

Such an atrocity is not typical. Nor does it de-legitimize the integrity of non-adoptive families. At the same time, Neha Afreen's murder by her father forcefully reminds us that all families, whether adoptive or non-adoptive, can be the sites of despair and even death for children.

In the same way that abuse perpetrated by birth parents does not and should not lead to a general indictment of non-adoptive families, instances of abuse by adoptive parents should not entail the denigration or even the demonization of adoption. To repeat what I said at the end of the previous chapter, we can all stipulate that children who lived in a fair and just world would grow up with birth parents in secure and nurturing homes. However, the homeless and abandoned children of 2013, like those throughout all the history we know, do not live in such a world, and never have. For many of them, the choices are between state care, no care at all, or adoption.

All adoptions, whether intra or intercountry, intra or interracial, entail disruption, loss, and mourning. At the same time, a long list of empirical

DOI: 10.1057/9781137333919

studies has demonstrated that adoption offers a substantially better outcome for abandoned children than the two alternatives that tend to
predominate in the countries in question: orphanages, and the street. I
have visited orphanages in several Asian countries; no child should be
denied the opportunity to escape such institutions.

So I return to the question of declining adoptions across borders.
While the increased capacity of some developing countries should
enable them to provide improved domestic care, including adoption,
for their children, there still remain millions of children throughout the
world whose lives are diminished, imperiled, and shortened by poverty,
abandonment, and abuse: children who might find a stable haven in a
family beyond the nation of their birth.

As Elizabeth Bartholet has said, "For most kids, the key negative is
not finding a home."[31] John Seabrook, introducing the story of the girl
he and his wife adopted from Haiti after the earthquake, said simply:
"We had never thought of ourselves as Rose's saviors. We wanted a child,
and Rose needed a family: it seemed like a fair trade."[32] There were an
estimated 380,000 orphans in Haiti before the disaster, and perhaps a
million immediately afterward. This in a total population of about ten
million.

Instead of a free-floating, contextless appeal to cultural solidarity, we
should consult the best interests of the child. Officials in most of the
world's nations agree. About one hundred countries have subscribed
to the Hague Convention (formal title: The Hague Convention on the
Protection of Children and Co-operation in Respect of Inter-Country
Adoption), which was concluded in 1993. Article 1A of the Convention
defines its primary purpose: to "establish safeguards to ensure that
inter-country adoptions take place in the best interests of the child...."
The best interests doctrine, whose origins we saw emerging in mid-
nineteenth-century New England, has now become a global standard.

Like all such international agreements, the Hague Convention has been
difficult to enforce.[33] Nonetheless, it has articulated and codified a set of
principles that governments and non-governmental humanitarian actors
and agencies can use to evaluate adoption practices around the world.

What about the claim that intercountry adoption allegedly threatens
the heritage and cultural identity of children? To begin with, children
who grow up in institutions or on the street will have little chance to
develop a meaningful cultural identity, at least not in any healthy sense.
The relevant research literature demonstrates that children adopted

DOI: 10.1057/9781137333919

across borders, like those adopted interracially, do not suffer dispropor-tionate harm to their sense of self. If they are adopted as infants, they thrive and fail at about the same rates as children who grow up in non-adoptive families. (Those adopted later, especially after long periods of time in institutions, do less well.)

But I want to go a bit further, and ask you to join me in examining the word "culture," which has from time to time played an important role in mobilizing opposition to intercountry adoption.

In Chapter 1, I quoted Raymond Williams's observation, in his book *Keywords*, that "nature" was perhaps the most complex word in the English language. In the same book, he opens his essay on "culture" by calling it "one of the two or three most complicated words" in the language. "I don't know how many times," he said some years later, "I've wished I'd never heard the damned word."[34]

Descending from the Latin, and signifying initially a process of car-ing for crops and animals, the word's meanings have multiplied across a dozen or more systems of reference. Societies and their sub-groups of clans and tribes possess culture; nations and regions, and the states, provinces, and sub-regions within them, also possess culture; ditto the various ethnic groups within each society and nation; the distinctive behaviors of academic disciplines are routinely described in cultural terms, and so are some of their productions—think of germ cultures; high culture is juxtaposed to mass culture or pop culture; consumer culture is a staple of journalism; for Matthew Arnold, culture was the antidote to anarchy; professional and amateur athletics evoke cultural descriptions. And so on.

The applications of "culture" are not merely multifarious. They are also—here is another likeness with "nature"—quite frequently contradic-tory. To quote Williams once more, within this array of meanings "there are fundamentally opposed as well as effectively overlapping positions; there are also, understandably, many unresolved questions and confused answers."[35]

Despite the confusion, "culture" has often been deployed in opposition to intercountry adoption, sometimes in the guise of the equally slippery term "heritage." Both words conceal at least as much as they reveal. Why should such elusive concepts as culture or heritage elicit automatic defer-ence? What is inherently valuable in these ideas?

To begin with, apart from the slogans of cultural ideologues, "cultural purity is an oxymoron." Living cultures, in Kwame Anthony Appiah's apt

DOI: 10.1057/9781137333919

formulation, are "inevitably, hybrid."³⁶ Salman Rushdie provides exuberant support, in a passage Appiah quotes. Rushdie declares that his great novel, *The Satanic Verses*

> celebrates hybridity, impurity, intermingling, the transformation that comes of new and unexpected combinations of human beings, cultures, ideas, politics, movies, songs. It rejoices in mongrelization and fears the absolutism of the Pure. Mélange, hotchpotch, a bit of this and a bit of that is how newness enters the world. It is the great possibility that mass migration gives the world, and I have tried to embrace it.

"Mass migration": while Rushdie almost certainly did not have inter-country adoption in mind, his kaleidoscopic defense of cultural contamination embraces those journeys as well.

While culture and nature are often presented as contraries, usually in Punch and Judy versions of human development, both abstractions provide camouflage for something less elevated: for what is familiar, what is taken for granted, for the way things are and have been. What is in this or that culture that commands conformity, or even respect? I fully understand the near-instinctive, perhaps even hard-wired, loyalty that binds individuals to their communities and (in the modern world) to their nations. Having invoked Franz Boas in Chapter 1, I trust it is clear that I fully endorse cultural latitudinarianism. Up to a point. Beyond which, it is transparently clear that cultural, ethnic, national, and local loyalties can and do lead to as much harm as good.

Out of deference to the alleged cultural autonomy of certain Hasidic Jews, the Brooklyn district attorney knowingly permitted years of child sexual abuse to continue without legal interference.³⁷ Roman Catholic women are denied ordination to the priesthood, and the women of some Jewish sects must undergo "purification" after childbirth—in both cases due to the power of sanctified customs. After deferring to the cultural priorities of Native American tribal law, federal and state officials belatedly intervened when they discovered evidence of long-standing patterns of child abuse on the Spirit Lake Indian Reservation in North Dakota. Even the man who has for years played Santa Claus is a registered sex offender.³⁸

Is there really such a thing as "the culture of football"? I can only report that a Google search using as keywords the terms "Penn State," "culture," and "football" yielded over 56 million hits. I scrolled through a couple of dozen items, all of which made the same predictable point: administrative

DOI: 10.1057/9781137333919

subservience to the "culture" of big-time athletics provided almost two decades of protection for the serial child rapist, Jerry Sandusky.

In Saudi Arabia, a woman cannot drive, must wear full-length coverings and veils in public, and cannot receive service in a restaurant unless a man accompanies her. These restraints are defended as intrinsic to the nation's religious culture and traditions. Indeed, even female genital mutilation has been defended on alleged cultural grounds, and outsiders who oppose the barbarous practice have occasionally been accused of some sort of ideological intrusion. As recently as 2005, the seventh case of *sati* was reported in one district in Uttar Pradesh since 1952. One journal called the widow's immolation on her husband's funeral pyre "a grim reminder of the endurance of a practice that should have long since been eradicated, and of the deep reverence that this crime still evokes among its believers."[39]

To put it summarily, all sorts of discrimination and brutality can be and have been validated by appeals to custom, or heritage, or tradition, or culture.

I mentioned earlier Pearl Buck's observation, decades ago, that opposition to intercountry adoption, when it appeals to "culture," re-traces with unintended irony the discredited preoccupation with "matching" that wrote children into and out of adoptability throughout much of the twentieth century. As we have seen, adoption has always posed a challenge to conventional assumptions about legitimacy, family integrity, inheritance, identity, and, yes, culture. Intercountry adoption raises those challenges with particular urgency. Such adoptions are emblematically connected to some of the most recurrent themes of twentieth and twenty-first-century experience across the globe: abandonment, displacement, homelessness, and exile. To the traditional anxiety associated with adoption, intercountry adoption adds the further complication of national and ethnic mixing. That symbolic valence perhaps explains why, despite the small numbers of individuals actually involved, intercountry adoption generates such lively debate, a debate that is often heated and sometimes even illuminating.

If misconceived invocations of culture (or heritage, tradition, custom) represent one threat to intercountry adoption, a different but related angle of attack has followed from nationalism, specifically from aggressive appeals to national pride. To put it simply, many nations—more accurately, the leaders of many nations—regard foreign adoption from their countries as a badge of dishonor. To permit one's children to be

DOI: 10.1057/9781137333919

removed to find homes across borders enacts a confession of domestic failure. Patriotism requires the assertion that the internal provision of child care is adequate, even when it is manifestly not adequate.[40]

Placing public relations concerns above the welfare of children, UNICEF and other organizations have promoted the idea that keeping children in the countries of their birth constitutes a self-justifying objective. No country wants to be charged with giving away or selling its own children—a fair enough concern when stated in such grotesque terms. However, intercountry adoption can be described in such terms only through a deliberate perversion of reality. Intercountry adoption, as I described earlier, has been abused and manipulated. However, the core of the practice, and its capacity for doing far more good than harm, remains untouched by instances of opportunism and greed.

Romania, Russia, China, Guatemala, Ecuador, and Peru are among the countries that have either suspended international adoption or imposed increasingly burdensome restrictions. These are also countries in which the alternatives for most homeless children reduce to life on the streets or institutional care in orphanages that are often unsafe, unsanitary, and unresponsive to their physical and emotional needs. Given the numbers of children at risk in these and other countries, even the temporary elimination of adoption consigns many boys and girls to diminished lives.

Those who argue that children must find care in their countries of birth should at least be candid in acknowledging two undeniable facts: first, that domestic adoption inside the borders of those countries is rarely going to happen; and second, that prolonged residence in institutions will inflict irreparable damage on many children. In a recent, graphic report for *The Times* of London, Rosa Monckton described what she found when she visited eight orphanages for young children in Bulgaria:

> It is the smell that assaults you—filthy nappies, unwashed babies, rotting flesh. Then you are hit by the silence, an eerie, unnatural silence, the silence of babies who have given up hope of ever being consoled, cuddled or comforted. It is the dreadful quiet of starving, neglected, unloved children waiting to die.
>
> The children in this particular wing have no human contact. They are fed lying on their backs, and have their nappies changed only when there happens to be a supply of new ones. Not one single word is uttered to them, so none of them is able to talk. This is how they live, and this is how they die.[41]

DOI: 10.1057/9781137333919

A 2009 study reports that the cessation of intercountry adoption has led to a sharp increase in the number of abandoned children in Vietnam, Guatemala, and Romania. According to the study,

> Now we have a Vietnamese report describing a "tide of unwanted newborns" overwhelming health care centers in Ho Chi Minh City, the largest city in the country.... What is tragic is that IA [international adoption] opponents last year proclaimed that the number of abandoned babies in Vietnam had risen because of the growth of International Adoption. Now International Adoption has ended and the number of abandoned babies continues to increase.[42]

All of us endorse and hope for improvements in the care available to young children in developing countries. However, given the record of failure in most countries in caring for abandoned and homeless children—I would emphatically include the United States in this assertion—fundamental reform will be a long time in coming.

Ignoring this simple humanitarian proposition, one critic of international adoption has asked, "Could it be argued that, rather than transferring the children of the poor to the economically better-off people in other countries, there should be a transfer of wealth from rich countries to poor ones?"[43] A statement like this is empty talk, with no connection to the politics of the real world in which poor children live. Worse, such an attitude holds children hostage to a posturing ideology. Given the scale of the crisis for children, and the efficacy of adoption as a strategy of intervention when—and I repeat only when—family preservation is impossible or unsafe for children, social policies should encourage an increase in the numbers of adoptions.

Obviously, the so-called traditional or nuclear family—two parents of the same race, one of each sex, married and living together with one or more birth children—no longer describes the American reality, if it ever did. Nonetheless, adoptive families, and especially mixed-race families, can still provoke confusion. In an odd alliance, some cultural conservatives, with their reverence for conventional norms, and some cultural theorists who fetishisize ethnic identity, join hands in finding mixed-race adoptive families subversive.

I would propose that we revise our ungenerous assumptions. Beyond its instrumental utility as a humanitarian intervention, international adoption exemplifies the possibility of re-orienting the definition of families away from either/or, monolithic ethnic and biological models. Families

DOI: 10.1057/9781137333919

really do come in all shapes and flavors. As Kwame Anthony Appiah has put it, describing Ghanaian family structure, and in doing so also summing up a thesis I have been proposing since I quoted the sentence in my prologue: "There are, in short, different ways of organizing family life."[44]

A 2000 federal law confers U.S. citizenship automatically on cross-border adoptees, once their adoption is finalized. This is undeniably a welcome reform, since it simplifies the lives of all concerned, and eliminates one of the anxious passages that used to accompany intercountry adoption.

However, there is also a loss in this advance. To be sure, Jennifer's application for citizenship in 1975 proved in many respects to be a kind of *opéra bouffe*. Three years old, she was obliged to testify that she had never been a member of subversive organizations, nor had she conspired to overthrow the American government. She also needed to secure two letters attesting to her good character (neither of which could be authored by her parents or siblings).

We kept as straight a collective face as we could through all these preliminary shenanigans, and we were unexpectedly rewarded. When Jennifer's application was approved, she was directed to appear in a federal courthouse in Philadelphia to take her oath. We found ourselves seated in a large hearing room, together with forty or so other about-to-be citizens, from almost as many countries, ranging in age from tiny children to the very old. The judge was himself an immigrant and a naturalized citizen who had come to America from Italy as a baby. Before administering the oath, he welcomed all his fellow immigrants, spoke eloquently about the ceremony, and then patiently called every name, asking each person called to stand up and accept our applause. Terry and I have rarely been so moved.

We have lived a richer life as a multi-ethnic adoptive family. And we have learned that such families are sites of constant ethnographic instruction. They offer routine access to cultural knowledge and experiences that lie outside the usual domestic interactions. Let me give, again from personal experience, just one example. After joining us, Jennifer quickly gained both pounds and facility in English. One night at dinner, when she was three years old, Jennifer suddenly announced: "Koreans don't eat broccoli." I also learned from my daughter that Koreans don't eat asparagus, or Brussels sprouts, either, though they do eat hot dogs and chocolate ice cream.

Who knew?

DOI: 10.1057/9781137333919

Notes

1 I have taken the phrase from J. A. S. Grenville, *A History of the World From the 20th to the 21st Century* (London: Routledge, 2005), p. 17.

2 Zbigniew Brzezinski, *Out of Control: Global Turmoil on the Eve of the Twentieth Century* (New York: Scribner, 1993), p. 10, xii.

3 Edward R. Kanowicz, *The Rage of Nations* (Grand Rapids, MI: Wm. B. Eerdmans Publishing Co., 1999), p. xv.

4 Tony Judt, *Postwar: A History of Europe since 1945* (New York: Penguin Press, 2005), pp. 20–21. See also Everett M. Ressler, Neil Boothby, and Daniel J. Steinbock, eds, *Unaccompanied Children: Care and Protection in Wars, Natural Disasters, and Refugee Movements* (New York: Oxford University Press, 1988), p. 9.

5 Frank Dikötter, *Mao's Great Famine: The History of China's Most Devastating Catastrophe, 1958–1962* (New York: Walker & Co., 2010), pp. 252–253. See also R. J. Rummel, *China's Bloody Century: Genocide and Mass Murder Since 1900* (New Brunswick, NJ: Transaction Publishers, 1991).

6 The United Nations defines an orphan as a child who has lost one or both parents.

7 UNICEF/UNAIDS, "Children and AIDS: Fifth Stocktaking Report" (2010). The nine countries are (in order of AIDS cases) Nigeria, South Africa, Tanzania, Uganda, Kenya, Zimbabwe, Zambia, Mozambique, and Malawi.

8 Emma Guest, *Children of AIDS: Africa's Orphan Crisis* (London: Pluto Press, 2001).

9 http://news.xinhuanet.com/english/2009–07/21/content_11745889.htm; http://www.nytimes.com/2002/07/21/nyregion/a-summer-of-hope-for-russian-orphans.html?pagewanted=all

10 Cited in Geoff Dyer, *The Missing of the Somme* (New York: Vintage Books, 2011 [1994]), p. 128.

11 A. M. Rosenthal, "Is This Still News?" *New York Times* (July 2, 1991), A17.

12 Robert E. Black, Saul S. Morris, Jennifer Bryce, "Where and Why are 10 Million Children Dying Each Year?" *The Lancet*, vol. 361, no. 9376 (June 28, 2003), pp. 2226–2234. The numbers have improved, but only slightly, in the decade since this report was published.

13 http://www.who.int/water_sanitation_health/hygiene/en/

14 Ishmael Beah, *A Long Way Gone: Memoirs of a Boy Soldier* (New York: Farrar, Straus and Giroux, 2007).

15 Sharon LaFraniere, "Africa's World of Forced Labor, in a 6-Year-Old's Eyes," *New York Times* (October 29, 2006), pp. 1, 16–17.

16 Christine Adamec and Laurie C. Miller, *The Encyclopedia of Adoption*, 3rd edn (New York: Facts on File, 2007), pp. 165–166.

DOI: 10.1057/9781137333919

17   Cited in Theodore F. Harris, *Pearl S. Buck: A Biography* (New York: The John Day Company, 1969), p. 299.

18   In the forty years between 1971 and 2011, upwards of half-a-million children came to the United States for adoption. See "International Adoption Facts," Evan B. Donaldson Adoption Institute <http://www.adoptioninstitute. org/FactOverview/international.html>, and "Intercountry Adoption," U.S. Bureau of Consular Affairs < http://adoption.state.gov/about_us/statistics. php>.

19   Robin Munro and Jeff Rigsby, *Death by Default: A Policy of Fatal Neglect in China's State Orphanages* (New York: Human Rights Watch, 1996), p. 260.

20   Karin Evans, *The Lost Daughters of China: Abandoned Girls, Their Journey to America, and the Search for a Missing Past* (New York: Putnam, 2000), p. 18.

21   Amartya Sen, "More Than 100 Million Women Are Missing," *The New York Review of Books* (December 20, 1990), pp. 61–66. Several demographers have proposed different figures, but estimates approximating Sen's original calculation have been widely accepted.

22   Valerie M. Hudson and Andrea M. den Boer, *Bare Branches: Security Implications of Asia's Surplus Male Population* (Cambridge, MA: The MIT Press, 2004), p. 264. There is much internal variation, by province in China, by state in India.

23   Apparently, the term was first used as the title of a book by Mary Anne Warren in 1985.

24   Maxine Hong Kinston, *The Woman Warrior: Memoirs of a Girlhood Among Ghosts* (New York: Vintage International, 1989 [1975]), pp. 46, 43.

25   http://www.who.int/mediacentre/factsheets/fs241/en/index.html

26   Barbara Crossette, "UNICEF is Fighting Violence Against Women," *New York Times* (March 9, 2000), A8; National Crime Records Bureau, "Disposal of Cases by Courts" <http://ncrb.nic.in/CII2008/cii-2008/Table%204.9.pdf>.

27   Sheela Rani Chunkath and V. B. Athreya, "Female Infanticide in Tamil Nadu: Some Evidence," *Economic and Political Weekly*, vol. 32, no. 17 (April 26–May 2, 1997), p. WS-28.

28   E. J. Graff, "Anatomy of an Adoption Crisis," *Foreign Policy* (September 12, 2010).

29   Mike Milotte, *Banished Babies: The Secret History of Ireland's Baby Export Business*, updated and expanded edition (Dublin: New Island, 2012).

30   *New York Times* (April 12, 2012), A7. No story beyond the caption accompanies the photograph.

31   Elizabeth Bartholet, "In the Best Interests of Children: A Permanent Family," a conference paper delivered in Guatemala City (January 20, 2005), p. 5.

32   John Seabrook, "The Last Babylift: Adopting a Child in Haiti," *The New Yorker* (May 10, 2010) <http://www.newyorker.com/ reporting/2010/05/10/100510fa_fact_seabrook>.

DOI: 10.1057/9781137333919

33   Richard Thompson Ford has formulated a provocative and skeptical counter-statement to what might be termed the universal human rights regime, which he calls "the dominant utopianism of our era." See *Universal Rights Down to Earth* (New York: W. W. Norton, 2011), p. 4. As his title suggests, Ford measures the distance between various declarations of human rights, all of them admirable in intent, and the actual behavior of many signatory countries. In his conclusion, Ford proposes that "the idea of human rights originated in natural-law theories that were religious in inspiration" (p. 122). As my discussion in Chapter 1 suggested, I believe that one can affirm human rights without appealing to natural law.

34   Raymond Williams, *Politics and Letters: Interviews with New Left Review* (London: New Left Books, 1979), p. 154.

35   Raymond Williams, *Keywords: A Vocabulary of Culture and Society*, revised edn (New York: Oxford University Press, 1983), p. 91.

36   Kwame Anthony Appiah, *Cosmopolitanism: Ethics in a World of Strangers* (New York: W. W. Norton & Company, 2006), pp. 113, 129.

37   These cases were widely reported. See, among many other reports, Sharon Otterman and Ray Rivera, "Ultra-Orthodox Shun Their Own for Reporting Child Sexual Abuse," *New York Times* (May 9, 2012). http://www.nytimes.com/2012/05/10/nyregion/ultra-orthodox-jews-shun-their-own-for-reporting-child-sexual-abuse.html?pagewanted=all

38   Timothy Williams, "Officials See Child Welfare Dangers on a North Dakota Indian Reservation," *New York Times* (July 7, 2012). http://www.nytimes.com/2012/07/08/us/child-welfare-dangers-seen-on-spirit-lake-reservation.html?pagew. See also Timothy Williams, "A Tribe's Epidemic of Child Sex Abuse, Minimized for Years," *New York Times* (September 19, 2012). http://www.nytimes.com/2012/09/20/us/us-steps-in-as-child-sex-abuse-pervades-sioux-tribe.html?pagewanted=all

39   "Enduring Practice," *Economic and Political Weekly* (June 11, 2005), p. 2372.

40   My comments in this section are informed by the work of Elizabeth Bartholet, most recently in her essay, "International Adoption: The Human Rights Position," *Global Policy*, vol. 1, no. 1 (January 2010), pp. 91–100.

41   Rosa Monckton, "Exposing Europe's Guilty Secret: The Incarcerated Children of Bulgaria," *The Times Online* (February 13, 2009) <http://www.timesonline.co.uk/tol/comment/columnists/article5720609.ece>

42   Center for Adoption Policy, "Newscap: What Happens When International Adoption Ends?" http://www.adoptionpolicy.org/archive/2009/may09.html. This and the previous quote are cited in part in Bartholet, "International Adoption," pp. 93–94.

43   Twila Perry, cited in David Eng, "Transnational Adoption and Queer Diasporas," *Social Text* (Fall, 2003), p. 10.

44   Kwame Anthony Appiah, *Cosmopolitanism*, p. 49.

DOI: 10.1057/9781137333919

5
Imagining Adoption

Conn, Peter. *Adoption: A Brief Social and Cultural History.* New York: Palgrave Macmillan, 2013.
DOI: 10.1057/9781137333919.

▶

DOI: 10.1057/9781137333919

As the example of Oedipus demonstrates, adoption has a centuries-long presence in the Western imagination. The dynamics and mysteries of kinship propel many imaginative texts, and adoption offers a singular entry into that familial complexity. Taking the word in a loose rather than a legal sense—that is to say, describing any situation in which children are separated from birth parents and grow up in alternative homes—British writing provides a large number of relevant texts, including Shakespeare's *Cymbeline* and *Pericles*, Jane Austen's *Mansfield Park*, Charlotte Brontë's *Jane Eyre*, several of Dickens's novels, among them *Bleak House*, *Oliver Twist*, *Great Expectations*, and *David Copperfield*, and George Eliot's *Adam Bede*, *Daniel Deronda*, and *Felix Holt*.[1]

American literature provides an even longer list of titles, beginning in the nineteenth century with Susan Warner's *The Wide, Wide World* (1851) and Susanna Maria Cummins's *The Lamplighter* (1854). American interest in adoption as a subject for fiction may follow from this country's distinctive attitude toward adoption itself. In my survey of adoptive practices in the United States, I suggested that the Old World's traditional and monarchical understanding of the family yielded to the more democratic conceptions of the New World. In short, America, that nursery of reinvention, would re-invent families as well as individuals.

Elaborating on the implications of this idea for imaginative literature, Carol Singley has proposed that the "adoption plot emerged as a literary form commensurate with and demonstrative of a new republican conception of the family as a nonhierarchical group of individuals whose will to be together is at least as important as blood ties .... The proliferation of adoption fiction occurred at a time when Americans were celebrating democratic individualism, freedom from English influence, and a sense of unlimited potential."[2]

That longstanding American interest in adoption as a fictional subject has become more widespread as adoption itself has become more common. As I mentioned earlier, millions of Americans now live in adoptive families, while others are considering adoption, and yet others are touched by adoption through friendship.

One (quite unscientific) index to that social transformation can be found in the growing number of novels and stories that take adoption as their premise. Recently, I searched the Library of Congress catalogue, using the subject heading: "adoptees—fiction." My search yielded about 120 English-language titles, of which over 90 have been published since the year 2000. In this chapter, I want to examine a dozen or so titles:

DOI: 10.1057/9781137333919

most (but not all) from the past decade, and most (but not all) from England and America. I have no homogenizing thesis to argue: fictional adoptions have proved to be as various and unpredictable as the real lives they represent. I will conclude with comments on a handful of adoption memoirs.

I begin with a glance at Christian Grey, who is—Oedipus and Tarzan and Harry Potter excepted—probably the most famous adopted character in fiction. Yes, I know: Christian's adopted status is not the reason for the astonishing popularity of *Fifty Shades of Grey* (2011). Nonetheless, Christian's adoption is in fact central to the novel's soft-core plot. His sexual preferences and physical demands have their sources in the ill treatment he suffered at the hands of his drug-addled birth mother and her boyfriend. Forced into submission as a child, he needs to have others accept submission in his adult relationships.

Like *Fifty Shades of Grey* and its two sequels, many of the adoption novels of the past decade have targeted the romance audience; their authors and their audiences are mainly women. Old habits and stereotypes die hard, and women are still more likely to provide the major readership for stories that have family relations at their center. Anna Adams's *Her Reason to Stay* (2008), about twin sisters separated by adoption, is published by Harlequin. Marisa Carroll's *Baby 101* (2000) is another Harlequin book, and Beverly Bird's *The Billionaire Drifter* (2003) appeared in the Silhouette series.

In Holly Chamberlin's *One Week in December* (2009), published under the romance imprint Kensington, Becca Rowan sets out to reclaim the daughter she gave up for adoption. Judy Christenberry's *A Texas Family Reunion* (2006), another Harlequin book, features a large cast and a complicated plot that revolves around the search for the members of a group of siblings orphaned and dispersed as children.

Nora Roberts, the phenomenally prolific author of over 200 romance novels, has used adoption as a plot mechanism on a number of occasions, most notably in her Chesapeake Series: *Sea Swept* (1998), *Rising Tides* (1998), *Inner Harbor* (1999), and *Chesapeake Blue* (2002).

The fact that these books make only modest claims on our aesthetic admiration is beside the point. These and the other titles I could identify—I have read about three dozen—document the reading public's lively interest in fictionalized versions of adoption as a subject. As critic William St. Clair recently reminded us, if we hope to make sense of a culture, we should take at least some account of "books that were actually read."[3] Books about adoption are being read.

DOI: 10.1057/9781137333919

Beyond that, the past decade has also brought more provocative adoption novels, books that engage the issues with considerable intelligence and skill. Let me provide a reader's guide to half-a-dozen or so.

Not surprisingly, Joyce Carol Oates, a tireless student of human dislocation and loss, has on several occasions taken adoption as her subject. In 1995, she published a one-act play, *The Adoption*, a slender satire directed at the narcissism of adoptive parents.[4] In the more recent and far more substantial *Mudwoman* (2012), pathology inheres in the birth family.

The novel alternates between the early 2000s and the 1960s and 1970s. The title character is Meredith Ruth Neukirchen—M.R., as she insists on being called—the first woman to be elected president of the unnamed Ivy League university at which she has been teaching philosophy. Gifted, energetic, and ambitious, she has spent her life trying to outrun the ghosts of her past. From her earliest childhood, she dimly recalls the sexual abuse she and her sister suffered at the hands of her mother's live-in boyfriend, who may also be their father.

When she was three years old, her mother had tried to murder her. Marit Kraeck, a religious fanatic, had thrown M.R. and her sister into the ooze of a mud flat on the edge of an impoverished, rural village in upstate New York. Both girls were intended as sacrifices of some sort, offerings to their deranged mother's lethal beliefs. "My mother wanted me to die," M.R. says to herself on several occasions, each time in surprise and disbelief.

The sister died (her mummified body is discovered years later). M.R. is rescued by a local trapper, placed first with a crowded, Dickensian foster family, then adopted by a Quaker couple, Konrad and Agatha Neukirchen, whose only child, a daughter, had died before her fourth birthday. Konrad works for the city government; Agatha is a librarian. With these people, Meredith knows for the first time the she lives in a "household in which, as in the most astonishing of fairly tales, she was beloved—whoever she was in this household, she was beloved. That she was Meredith Ruth—'Merry'—she would never want for love."[5]

From this house, in a town called Carthage, M.R. begins her ascent: a scholarship to Cornell, a fellowship to Harvard, then a professorship, and eventually the presidency of an elite New Jersey university in her early forties. (The university, never named, is a barely disguised Princeton.) While the presidency may bring her occasional satisfaction, we see nothing but M.R.'s pain: her self-doubts and anxieties, her exhaustion,

DOI: 10.1057/9781137333919

her discomfort in the inevitable, interminable, and stupefyingly dull meetings that demand her daily attendance.

A liberal academic, she bridles at the political neutrality demanded of a modern college president. Above all, she hates the courtship rules that oblige her to treat with respect wealthy people whose politics she despises. In one hugely improbable sequence, she turns down a $35 million donation because she deems the donor immoral. She lives alone in the grand mausoleum that is the president's house, yearning for a visit (or even a phone call) from her secret lover, a Harvard astronomer, a man fifteen years older than she, married unhappily to a woman he will not leave. M.R.'s sleep is maimed by nightmare visions of rape, murder, and dismemberment, episodes that Oates narrates as if they had actually occurred.

The novel takes us only through the first year of M.R.'s term: a sequence of larger and smaller gaffes and mis-steps that culminates in a three-month medical leave of absence. The last few chapters offer a glimpse of something better. M.R. returns to Carthage, to her childhood home. Here she finds consolation. Agatha, who had spent years refusing to consult doctors for her various ailments, has died. Konrad, to whom M.R. was always especially close, provides the consolation she desperately needs, and the humane wisdom she had never found in the abstractions of academic philosophy.

M.R.'s equilibrium is threatened once more before the novel ends. Learning from Konrad that her birth mother had been incarcerated in a hospital for the criminally insane and might still be alive, M.R. decides that she must see her. Konrad is dubious.

> "I suppose you could see her—if that is your wish."
> If that is your wish. How like a fairy-tale warning this was!

As soon as she arrives at the hospital, she knows this is a dreadful error: "M.R. felt a stab of terror, she was making a mistake to have come here and what would this mistake be but one of a concatenation of mistakes, foolish blunders that had ruined her life."

The reunion is a fiasco. Her mother shuffles painfully into the visiting area, dressed in a stained, shapeless dress, smelling of "dried sweat, urine, feces." Nearly brain-dead with the sedatives poured into her each day by the staff, Marit offers M.R. absolutely no sign of recognition. Appalled by finding what she knew she would find, "M.R. wanted to hide her eyes, like a child in a fairy tale exposed to a forbidden sight." She hurries from the room, never to return.

DOI: 10.1057/9781137333919

The repeated invocations of fairy tales is of course vintage Oates: reminding us that in her fictional world demons and goblins always lurk in the shadows of happiness, where they plot to overwhelm whatever contentment or even stability her characters may find. A few days after the scarifying scene with Marit, and in the novel's last line, M.R. returns to the university. Whether she will find some sort of redemption or collapse in a final humiliation we never learn.

Talking about the sources of *Mudwoman* with a reporter, Oates pointed out the similarities between her main character and herself:

> We all know that everything in a dream is an aspect of ourselves, and so I recognized this Mudwoman as an aspect of myself. My background is a little like M.R.'s—not so desperate, not so poor, but still the world of poverty that surrounded me as a child—and when I go back to my home town, I have a visceral feeling of excitement, but also dread, as if there's a secret memory that I've forgotten, that maybe it was good for me to forget—as if I'll remember something I shouldn't remember.

Nowhere in her autobiographical comments does Oates mention the most obvious difference between M.R. and herself, which is at once the most important fact in M.R.'s story. Oates's parents were working class but stable and reliable. M.R. was abandoned and then adopted, finding in her alternative family the affection and support that her birth mother had brutally denied her.

Thirty years before the appearance of *Mudwoman*, P. D. James published *Innocent Blood* (1980), a novel that also has a murderous birth mother lurking at its center. Philippa Palfrey is the adoptive daughter and only child of an urbane, high-profile London academic named Maurice, and his second wife and former secretary, Hilda, a woman trapped in insecurity and perpetual disappointment. Philippa was adopted when she was seven years old, and has grown restive in the conventional care of her conventional parents. She nurses the fantasy that her mother was a servant in an aristocratic household, and her father was a nobleman.

Within days of her eighteenth birthday, authorized by the Children's Act of 1975, which has opened adoption records, she sets out in search of her birth mother. What she discovers is that this woman, Mary Ducton, has spent the years since Philippa's adoption in prison, convicted of murdering a twelve-year-old girl, Julia Scase, whom her husband Martin had raped. Martin has died in jail, but Mary is about to be released on

DOI: 10.1057/9781137333919

parole. Ignoring Maurice's warnings, and insisting on the primacy of the "blood tie," Philippa befriends her mother and rents a small apartment for them in a shabby London neighborhood. Unknown to Philippa and Mary, Julia's father Norman has been following them, intent on murdering Mary in revenge for his daughter's death.

The novel's final crisis occurs when Philippa learns that Mary had given her up *before* Julia's murder. More precisely, Philippa was removed from Mary after she threw her daughter down a set of stairs and fractured her skull. Realizing that her mother never wanted her, Philippa denounces Mary and leaves the apartment. When she returns the following day, she finds Norman Scase collapsed over the dead body of her mother. But Scase hasn't killed Mary; in a coincidence worthy of a Victorian melodrama, she had poisoned herself shortly before Scase's arrival.

When she began her search, a social worker had warned Philippa: "We all have our fantasies in order to live. Sometimes relinquishing them can be extraordinarily painful, not a rebirth into something exciting and new but a kind of death."[6] So it proves to be in this novel, in which truth brings only sorrow and regret.

Set in San Francisco, in 1974–1975, Ellen Ullman's remarkable *By Blood* (2012) is suffused with bad weather and a ubiquitous dread:

> Oil crisis, unemployment, stagflation, a fruitless war in Vietnam slowly coming to an end. San Francisco seemed a dark and frightening place. Patty Hearst's kidnapping. White people all over the city had been murdered in the Zebra killings. The Zodiac serial killer was still at large.

And later:

> Adding to it all, a report that braved the static of my radio: an atomic submarine that had released radioactive waste onto the beaches of Guam, fifty times the supposedly safe dosage, which spoke...of a despaired world where we human beings were doomed to destroy ourselves, and everything else along with us.[7]

In one of the city's seedier neighborhoods, on the eighth floor of a nondescript office building, a thirty-year-old woman, never named, is seeing a therapist, a German immigrant named Dr. Dora Schlosser. Most of the novel's 125 brief chapters record the discussions that take place in each therapeutic session. The "patient," as she is called, has come to Dr. Schlosser ostensibly for help in managing her relationship with her

DOI: 10.1057/9781137333919

lesbian partner, a woman named Charlotte. Dr. Schlosser presses the patient to go beyond her current troubles, to reach back and discuss her feelings about being adopted. The patient resists; the doctor keeps pushing; the patient finally agrees.

The tangled story that the patient discovers makes up the bulk of the chapters: each session adding another bit of information or surmise. The narrative does not come to the reader directly. Instead, it is all reported by an eavesdropper who occupies the office next to the therapist, and can overhear every word through the thin wall. This man, also never named, is a college professor who has been forced to take a leave of absence while his university investigates allegations of sexual misconduct with an undergraduate. ("Creep. Letch. Pervert. That's what the students...had called me.")

He not only listens; he intervenes, undertaking research which he surreptitiously provides the patient, leads that eventually enable her to track down her birth mother. Though he insists that he was only trying to be helpful, this secret sharer is a surpassingly revolting character: paranoid, filled with self-loathing, ingesting the patient's confessions with the relish of a vampire lapping up blood. The entire narrative apparatus is contrived, implausible, and yet irresistible: a tour de force that compels the reader to share in repeated acts of violation.

The search for the patient's origins ultimately leads from California to Israel, from the 1970s to the 1940s, from the lesser apocalypse of the present to the far greater calamity of the Holocaust.

The patient, who has been raised by Protestant parents, discovers that she was born in the Bergen-Belsen concentration camp, the child of a Jewish mother named Micah Gerson who gave her up for adoption at the end of the war. Aided unknowingly by the narrator, who has sent information under the guise of an officer at one of the adoption agencies she has contacted, the young woman travels to Jaffa, where she finds her birth mother, and also finds the older sister she did not know she had.

Who was her birth father? In the novel's most astonishing revelation, the young woman learns that her Aryan-looking mother had been housed for some time in a special, quite comfortable maternity hospital. Here she had been obliged to accept Nazi men as sexual partners, as part of Heinrich Himmler's *Lebensborn* program, a reproductive scheme to provide the next generation of Nazis. Both the young woman and her sister may have been conceived by their mother with a German officer.

DOI: 10.1057/9781137333919

Thus the dream of discovery and reunion is displaced by the nightmare of possible Nazi parentage: the novel's title, *By Blood*, takes on bitterly ironic implications. The young woman may have been the by-product of the Nazis' demonic desire to create a pure-blooded Aryan super-race. The irony is deepened by the fact that the patient's therapist, Dr. Schussler, is the daughter of an SS officer, a "true believer in the Fuhrer and the Master Race." This secret, vouchsafed only to the narrator and the reader, explains Schussler's obsession with parental origins.

The truth can sometimes confer more pain than consolation.

Ellen Ullman is adopted. Or, as both she and the unnamed patient of *By Blood* put it, "I am not adopted; I have mysterious origins." Referring to open adoptions and the right to know, she says, "I am not against this trend. I simply want to give not-knowing its due .... I like mysteries. I like the sense of uniqueness that comes from having unknown origins."

Before turning to novel writing, Ullman made a successful career as a computer programmer: a pioneering choice for a woman in Silicon Valley in the 1970s. She credits the engineers and math professors in her adoptive family for making that vocation possible and desirable. When she thought about her birth parents, she conjured "actresses, folk singers, writers and intellectuals." Under their tutelage, she would not have found her place in what she calls "the defining profession of my time." And she adds, "I could just see my birth mother looking up from George Eliot's *Daniel Deronda* (Book V, 'Mordecai') to say, 'Darling, why struggle so on those cold programs when you haven't yet read *Middlemarch*?' "[8]

A long-secret adoption also provides one of the major plot devices in Elie Wiesel's *The Sonderberg Case* (2010). The main character, Yedidayah Wasserman, is the anguished descendant of Holocaust survivors. He wants to be an actor, a shape-shifting profession that would let him escape the question of his own identity. Persuaded that he doesn't have the talent for performing, he becomes a semi-successful theater critic for a New York paper. Yedidayah's life changes when he is assigned to cover a sensational murder trial. The young German immigrant Werner Sonderberg, a brilliant student of comparative literature at NYU, has been charged with the murder of his uncle, Hans Dunkelman, who was found dead at the bottom of a cliff in the Adirondacks where the two men had been hiking.

The trial—and the novel—take a remarkable twist when Sonderberg pleads "guilty ... and not guilty." Before he can testify, the case is thrown

DOI: 10.1057/9781137333919

out for lack of evidence. Twenty years after the trial, Wasserman and Sonderberg meet. We learn that Dunkelman was not Sonderberg's uncle but his paternal grandfather, a fugitive Nazi war criminal living under an assumed name. He has sought out his grandson to tell him, pridefully, about his role as an enthusiastic murderer in the camps. Denounced by Werner, and driven to despair, the older man had thrown himself off the cliff. It is an implausible turn in the story, but the dialogue that precedes it includes a warning about allegiance to ties of blood.

Recalling the atrocities of Treblinka and Birkenau, which he had supervised, the elder Sonderberg insists:

> "It was simple and implacable in this cursed place, the condemned had come to die and I had come to kill. At no time was I seized with remorse or pity. I saw everything, I retained everything. I thought it was necessary. That is was just."
>
> Motionless, horrified, Werner cried out angrily, "'And you want me to be proud of being related to you?"
>
> "Whether you like it or not, you are. By blood."
>
> "Well, blood can lie. In our case, it lies. You and I, we don't belong to the same human family."
>
> "There again, whether you like it or not, we're related; we're relatives."
>
> "Then I'll bear this kinship like a burden. Worse—like a curse."[9]

In counterpoint with the Sonderberg case, Wiesel explores what might be called the Wasserman case. Throughout the novel, Yedidayah has brooded on his own past: what does he know about the people he has called Father, and Mother, and Grandfather? More important, what doesn't he know?

Two-thirds of the way through the book, Yedidayah tells us: "It may be time to reveal that my grandfather, the man whom I loved so dearly, is not my grandfather; Rabbi Petahia is not my ancestor; my parents are not my parents. Mine are dead. The enemy killed them when I was an infant."

He had been the younger of two brothers. When the round-up of Jews began in the village, a Christian peasant woman from a nearby town took him to her home and hid him, saving his life. After the war, this woman, Maria Petrescu, made contact with one of the agencies that tried to reunite Jewish families or find Jewish homes for orphans.

DOI: 10.1057/9781137333919

In dreams, Yedidayah reaches out to his dead family. His most important exchange is with his mother. He asks:

> "Did you love me before …"
> "Before what?"
> "Before abandoning me?"
> "Before saving you, you mean. Yes I loved you. I loved you gently, passionately for the rest of your life" (p. 147).

In an earlier chapter, reaching into medieval European history, I described the use of abandonment to rescue children. Wiesel's novel re-enacts that history in a later generation.

Aimee Phan has written about Operation Babylift in a collection of interconnected stories, *We Should Never Meet* (2004). The eight stories alternate between South Vietnam at the time of the war's ending, and America in the years that followed. Phan captures the confusion and fear of Vietnamese parents who contemplate giving up their children to protect them from Viet Cong reprisals. Phan also offers portraits of four of the children as they grow to maturity in America.

In the final story, "Motherland," a young man named Huan, half Vietnamese, half African-American, reluctantly agrees to re-visit Vietnam with his adoptive family. Huan is caught between conflicting emotions of gratitude and bitterness over the outcome of his life. He knows that his white parents love him, but he is angry that his life's course was shaped by an eruption of violence that no child should have to suffer.

In Saigon, now Ho Chi Minh City, Huan meets a friend, Mai, another Vietnamese orphan whose life has taken her away from her native land. Thinking back on the Vietnamese parents who gave their children up for adoption, Mai says

> "I was afraid of hating everyone here …."
> "How do you feel now?" Huan asks.
> "I know better. It's not our parents' fault. Or anyone else's here. How could I be angry with them, expect them to do right when there was no such thing? When everything here was wrong?"
> Huan nods, understanding. It was a war.
> It was.[10]

Mai knows that war inevitably brings chaos and damage, and that children will always find themselves in harm's way. She knows that she and

DOI: 10.1057/9781137333919

Huan and thousands of other abandoned and orphaned children were referred to as *bui doi*, the dust of life, part of the collateral damage that is always inflicted on the most vulnerable in times of violence.

Two generations of adoption anchor the plot of Chang-rae Lee's novel, *A Gesture Life* (1999). Seventy-year-old Franklin Hato is a Korean immigrant who has made a new life in an affluent New York City suburb called Bedley Run. As a young boy, he was (somewhat implausibly) adopted from his Korean Oh family and raised by a childless Japanese couple who re-named him Jiro Kurohata. He did well in school, but his plans to become a doctor were scuppered by the onset of the war. He enlisted as a low-ranking medical orderly, loyally serving "his" emperor and Japan's imperial cause.

After the war, Hata moved to the U.S., changed his name, and built a good business in medical supplies. He lives in a large house on one of the most desirable streets in Bedley Run. Over the years, "Doc" Hata has become a respected member of his community, widely consulted by others on matters large and small, never the target of discrimination or insult. Recently retired, he is treated with "almost Oriental veneration as an elder."[11]

Outwardly, his quiet life is a model of American success. Hata's inner life, on the other hand, is the scene of a constant struggle against the crippling memories of what he saw and did in the war. Armored in a rigorous decorum and tidiness, he finds his thoughts frequently disrupted by the wartime horrors that have permanently marked him. A lifelong bachelor, Hata has adopted a Korean orphan, a girl he rather hopefully calls Sunny. His attempt at fatherhood is an effort to fill the void that the war has maimed his life.

His relationship with Sunny almost immediately turns sour. She realizes that her adoption had little to do with her needs, and she bridles under his silent but relentless discipline. He wants her to excel in her schoolwork and her music. She is also repelled by Hata's cautious daily routines:

> All I've ever seen is how careful you are with everything. With our fancy big house and this store and all the customers. How you sweep the sidewalk and nice-talk to the other shopkeepers. You make a whole life out of gestures and politeness. You're always having to be the ideal partner and colleague. (p. 95)

Sunny's judgment is correct, though she cannot know the sources of Hata's carefully orchestrated existence. Having witnessed the most

DOI: 10.1057/9781137333919

extreme violence, Hata has learned how vulnerable human beings are, how easily destroyed. His efforts to protect Sunny from dangers and temptations, which are rooted in his own experience, seem to her merely acts of control. She leaves his house as a teenager and only at the end of the novel, more than a decade later, she now the single mother of a mixed-race son, do they inch toward reconciliation.

The suburban tranquility of Bedley Run lies an immeasurable distance from the East Asian military camp to which Hata was posted in the war's latter stages. Pulverized by heat, disease, and tension, the encampment is a place of dwindling supplies and shrinking morale. The commander has collapsed into drugged incompetence, his authority exercised by a sadistic medical officer, Captain Ono. Everyone waits for an attack that never comes. The fearful tedium is relieved only by the arrival of five "comfort women," the euphemism used to describe the young Korean girls and women forced to provide sexual service to the camp's 200 men.

The horrific treatment to which these women are subjected provides the novel's most graphic scenes. Torn between loyalty to his superiors and his own anguished decency, Hata tries to save one of the women from degradation. His ultimate failure—she is killed in a prolonged gang rape that Hata is powerless to stop—proves to be the decisive event of his life. Having made the mistake of falling in love with a woman murdered before his eyes, Hata lives the remainder of his life through carefully managed gestures.

As the novel moves back and forth between Asia and America, between the dark unburied past and the apparently sunlit present, key images recur that link Hata's two worlds. In the camp, he had witnessed a medical experiment in which Captain Ono slices open the chest of a still-living Burmese peasant to demonstrate resuscitation techniques. Decades later, a young boy lies dying in a Bedley Run hospital, waiting for a heart transplant. An orgiastic party at which Sunny dances provocatively for a group of drunken men recalls the bestial sexual behavior of the Japanese soldiers. For Hata, to paraphrase Faulkner, the past isn't dead or even past.

Lee has said that the novel began with the comfort women: "I originally wanted to write a book that was told from the point of view" of one of these women. Deciding that he needed a witness rather than a victim as the novel's center, he eventually created Franklin Hata.

In telling the stories of these intertwined lives, Lee deploys adoption as an emblem of displacement. Born to Koreans, Franklin Hata grew up

DOI: 10.1057/9781137333919

as Japanese, and spends most of his life as an American. Abandoned by her Korean parents, Sunny grows up in America. Both father and daughter have been wounded by events far beyond their control or even their understanding. Both are marginal figures by circumstance and choice. At the end of the novel, Hata has decided to sell his big house but hasn't decided where he will go:

> Let me simply bear my flesh, and blood, and bones. I will fly a flag. Tomorrow, when this house is alive and full, I will be outside looking in. I will be already on a walk someplace, in this town or the next or one five thousand miles away. I will circle round and arrive again. Come almost home. (p. 356).

It is a poignant close to a harrowing life.

April Epner, the thirty-something protagonist of Elinor Lipman's novel, *Then She Found Me* (1990), harbors no romantic illusions about her birth parents:

> My biological mother was seventeen when she had me in 1952, and even that was more than I wanted to know about her. I had no romantic notions about the coupling that had produced me, nor about her being cheerleader to his football captain or au pair to his Rockefeller. When I thought about it at all, this is what I imagined: two faceless and cheap teenagers doing it listlessly in the unfinished basement where they jitterbugged unchaperoned.[12]

April had been adopted at six months by a Jewish couple, Gertrude and Julius Epner, Holocaust survivors building a new life in the United States. They chose adoption because Gertrude believed she had lost her fertility in the camps.

From her adoptive parents, April had learned to be serious, realistic, and honest. But she has not learned much about joy. At the time of the novel's events, in the mid-1980s, both Gertrude and Julius have recently died. The still-single April is teaching Latin in a public high school near Boston, reasonably content in a low-keyed sort of way.

Enter Bernice Graverman, the "she" of the novel's title, who has kept tabs on April from a distance and decides, after more than three decades, to re-enter her life. A local television celebrity, the host of a confessional talk show—"Bernie G!"—with a large female audience, Bernice is a wonderful comic creation, a swashbuckling, female Falstaff: narcissistic, rapaciously needy, opportunistic, incapable of telling the truth, and altogether irresistible. She first tells April that her biological father was John

DOI: 10.1057/9781137333919

F. Kennedy, who swept Bernice off her feet in a brief affair. Later, she will claim that the father was not Jack Kennedy but Jack Kerouac.

Initially appalled by the human tidal wave that has disrupted her sober existence, April eventually succumbs to Bernice's madcap charm. The novel's plot, which traces a frankly sentimental trajectory toward reconciliation, is less striking than its generous and often funny tone, which in the end rescues the book.

Along with a number of distinguished novels and stories, adoption has also provided material for countless memoirs. Many are sentimentally predictable—the non-fiction kin of the Harlequin and Silhouette romances I mentioned earlier. However, some of these narratives of personal discovery and re-appraisal match talent with ambition. Three books, one American, the other two British, will offer examples.

American novelist A. M. Homes always knew she was adopted. She knew that when she was born, in 1961, her birth mother was young and unmarried. She also knew that her birth father was older and married. For three decades, that was all the information she had. Then, in December, 1992, her adoptive mother told her that her birth mother had finally decided to "get in touch." Homes, who had spent her life in what she calls a kind of witness protection program, is suddenly faced with the possibility of learning more, a great deal more, with consequences that she knows will be unpredictable. *The Mistress's Daughter* (2007) records the events that followed, and Homes's efforts to find room in her life for a second narrative:

> ...the thin line of story, the plot of my life, has been abruptly recast. I am dealing with the divide between sociology and biology: the chemical necklace of DNA that wraps around the neck sometimes like a beautiful ornament—our birthright, our history—and other times like a choke chain.[13]

While she is confident of her adoptive parents' love, Homes has sometimes dreamed of the superior woman her birth mother might be: a goddess, a queen, the CEO, the CFO, and the COO. Her birth mother is surely "movie-star beautiful, incredibly competent," a woman who "can take care of anyone and anything. She has made a fabulous life for herself, as ruler of the world ..." (p. 9).

The truth turns out to be sadly different. Ellen Ballman teeters on the edge of poverty, lumbered with a police record, and suffering from

DOI: 10.1057/9781137333919

a serious kidney disease for which she is too frightened to seek treatment. (She will die before the story closes.) When she and Homes begin talking—initially only on the phone, at Homes's insistence—Ballman nearly overwhelms her birth daughter with her own neediness:

> "Why won't you see me?" she whines. "You're torturing me. You take better care of your dog than you take of me."
>
> Am I supposed to be taking care of her? Is that what she's come back for?
>
> "You should adopt me—and take care of me," she says.
>
> "I can't adopt you," I say.
>
> "Why not?"
>
> I don't know how to respond. (p. 33)

After several "terrifying" conversations along these lines, Homes concludes that "the more Ellen and I talk, the happier I am that she gave me up. I can't imagine having grown up with her. I would not have survived" (p. 34). Ballman stalks her, calls constantly, shows up at one of Homes's book readings, and in general becomes a figure of dread to her daughter. Their few meetings are fiascos.

The disillusion of re-connecting with her birth mother is doubled when Homes meets her (probable) birth father. Three decades earlier, Norman Hecht had seduced Homes's seventeen-year-old mother, kept her as his mistress for several years, then simply abandoned her when Ellen Ballman became pregnant. He demands that Homes take a DNA test (though he never tells her the result). He refuses to tell his wife and children about this daughter. When they meet, furtively, in hotel lounges or restaurants, Homes imagines that he wants to see her naked, wants her to become his second-generation mistress. In Homes's exquisitely precise one-word summary, Norman Hecht is a jerk.

Homes learns what there is to know about her birth parents almost immediately, and her disconcerting revelations take us only through the book's first quarter or so. The remainder is filled with her obsessive search to find out all that she can about both Ellen Ballman and Norman Hecht. She spends days and weeks in libraries, subscribes to several online genealogical search services, hires research assistants, and interviews dozens of aging men and women who might be able to fill in the blanks.

Homes expands her search to include her adoptive parents as well. She finds out a great deal about these four people, though much of it is

DOI: 10.1057/9781137333919

more or less hypothetical. She also learns a more general lesson. Looking around her at the dozens of other seekers in the New York City archives, she realizes that "they're not all adopted...I remind myself that the quest to answer the question 'Who am I?' is not unique to the adoptee" (p. 152).

The Mistress's Daughter is marred from time to time by tactless grandiosity. On one occasion, watching *Schindler's List*, Homes calls the film's tragedy "equal to what I am feeling." Shortly afterwards, she says she feels like "a white, female Martin Luther King Jr." (pp. 79, 91). The search for her past may be serious, but the stakes are not as high as that. To be sure, adoption can be disorienting, but A. M. Homes has evidently found her way productively forward.

Indeed, in the book's final and most moving section, "My Grandmother's Table," Homes pays extended and loving tribute to her adoptive grandmother:

> Jewel Rosenberg, my grandmother, my adoptive mother's mother, graceful, grandiloquent, profound. She is in some ways why or how this book exists. I am not sure that I would have become a writer if it weren't for her, nor would I have gone to such lengths to become a mother (p. 225).

The child of immigrants, born in 1900 in northern Massachusetts, Jewel in her eighties and nineties, after a lifetime of productive work, had become the matriarch, the repository of wisdom, the woman who always sat, literally and figuratively, at the head of the table. "Whatever I know about how to live my life," Homes tells us, "I learned from her" (p. 232).

Happy families may or may not all be happy in the same way—I'm fairly sure Tolstoy got that part wrong—but unhappy families are indeed unhappy in different ways, none more differently or weirdly than Jeannette Winterson's. She told the story in an autobiographical first novel, *Oranges Are Not the Only Fruit* in 1985, and returns to it in her 2012 memoir, *Why Be Happy When You Could Be Normal?*

Given up for adoption at eleven days old by her bewildered and penniless unwed mother, Winterson grew up in a working class cottage in Accrington, a hardscrabble town twenty miles north of Manchester. The house was two-up, two-down, with no phone, an outdoor water closet, and a coal hole. The family was dominated by a cold, unloving, and probably clinically deranged Bible-thumping mother, Constance, a Pentecostal fanatic usually identified throughout this memoir as "Mrs. Winterson," presumably to keep her at arm's length.

DOI: 10.1057/9781137333919

Winterson's adoptive father is a laborer and the sole source of family income. But he is a minor figure in the house, taciturn, permanently exiled from the marital bed, a shadowy figure who seems less a human being than a piece of the threadbare furniture in the cottage.

Mrs. Winterson, on the contrary, is a force of nature, emotionally smothering, and dangerous into the bargain: she keeps a revolver in the duster drawer and bullets in an old tin of Pledge. Jeannette calls her a "flamboyant depressive... suffering was the meaning of her life."[14] She weighs nearly 300 pounds and is large enough to fill a phone box: "She was out of scale, larger than life. She was like a fairy story where size is approximate and unstable. She loomed up. She expanded" (p. 36).

Her waking hours are filled with prayer, Bible reading, and hymns. She loves Jesus but hates the world and everything and everybody in it, including herself. Every day she prayed, "Lord, let me die." When she loses her temper at Jeannette, which she often does, she tells her that "The Devil led us to the wrong crib" (p. 1). In one of the book's funniest and scariest set pieces, Winterson recalls walking with her mother down the town's main street, where a sink of depravity lurks behind every storefront:

We went past Woolworth's—"A Den of Vice." Past Marks and Spencer's— "The Jews Killed Christ." Past the funeral parlor and the pie shop—"They share an oven." Past the biscuit stall and its moon-faced owners— "Incest." Past the pet parlor—"Bestiality." Past the bank—"Usury." Past the Citizens Advice Bureau—"Communists." Past the day nursery—"Unmarried mothers." Past the hairdresser's—"Vanity" (pp. 86–87).

Mrs. Winterson inadvertently provided the book's title. After subjecting the teen-aged Jeannette to an exorcism in a failed effort to cure her sexual attraction to women, Mrs. Winterson asks, in what seems to be genuine puzzlement: "Why be happy when you could be normal" (p. 114)?

Mrs. Winterson may be a monster, to use one of her daughter's epithets, a grotesque out of fairy tale or nightmare, but she is by far the most memorable figure in the memoir. Radiating energy like an exploding star, her ranting obsessions vivify what is otherwise a self-absorbed portrait of the writer as young woman. Put briefly, Mrs. Winterson is far more interesting than her daughter. The book weakens in its latter sections, when the daughter's sermons and low-rent philosophizing about books and religion displace the manic mother.

DOI: 10.1057/9781137333919

The book concludes with Jeannette's successful search for her birth mother, a story that alternates with a brief history of the assorted therapeutic remedies she sought out. She learns that her mother's name is Ann S., and they meet in Ann's living room in a Manchester suburb. The meeting is cordial but touches no deep place: while Ann wants to include her birth daughter in her family, Jeannette immediately decides that "I don't want to be there. That's not what's important to me. And I don't feel a biological connection. I don't feel, 'Wow, here's my mother'" (p. 229).

Furthermore, Jeannette finds herself bridling at Ann's harsh appraisals of (the now deceased) Mrs. Winterson: "I notice that I hate Ann criticizing Mrs. Winterson. She was a monster but she was my monster" (p. 229). Mrs. Winterson's eccentricity, verging on madness, propelled Jeannette to escape. And in the end,

> I would rather be this me—the me that I have become—than the me I might have become without books, without education, and without all the things that have happened to me along the way, including Mrs. W. I think I am lucky. (p. 228)

Jeremy Harding's *Mother Country* (2010) is not merely, as its subtitle describes it, the "memoir of an adopted boy." This warm-hearted, humane, and beautifully written book transforms Harding's quest for his birth mother into a distilled social history of England in the second half of the twentieth century. A meditation on memory, class, and kinship, and suffused with humor and compassion, the book assembles an ever-growing cast of characters in a riveting detective story.

Harding was five when he learned that he was adopted, and he never found that fact problematic or even particularly interesting. Rather than seeing his adoption as a "primal wound,"[15] in the over-heated formula of one writer, Harding felt no trauma at all. "It wasn't obvious to me that the blood tie mattered," he writes in the introduction he provided for his book's American edition. "I liked to think that if families worked, it was because they'd gone about inventing themselves in the right way, which was largely a question of luck."[16]

Eventually, in part because the middle-aged Harding felt that his children might have some curiosity about their biological past, he set out to see what he might be able to find out about the woman who had borne him, and then given him up for adoption when he was a few days old. All he has, to begin with, is a name: Maureen Walsh. He brings to the task his formidable skills as a seasoned investigative journalist. The internet helps, but most of

DOI: 10.1057/9781137333919

what Harding seeks still lurks outside the edges of the digital world. So he spends hours and days tracking possible leads through the musty, hand-written ledgers of public registry offices in and around London.

In the course of recording the search for his birth mother, Harding spends even more time recalling the mother and father who had in fact been his mother and father, the couple who had adopted and raised him. The strongest parts of the book are those in which middle-aged Harding morphs into young Jeremy Harding, living throughout his childhood in a variety of Thames-side cottages. His adoptive mother, Maureen, emerges as the book's most memorable character. For years, she had regaled her only child with stories of her affluent background, the big house she lived in as a girl, the expensive dresses she wore, the carriages in which she rode, the elegant dalmatians that lent doggy glamor to her early life.

None of it, as Harding discovers in the course of his search, is true. Maureen has invented herself as the privileged character she wished she had been. With an almost implausible symmetry, Maureen's favorite record is the soundtrack from *My Fair Lady*, a recording of which she played again and again on the gramophone. While he scrupulously corrects his mother's self-portrait, he treats her with affection and even respect: Maureen, after all, was merely trying to escape the heavy burden of the English class system. Who wouldn't? In any case, as a writer of great resource, Harding knows that the facts of names and dates often tell us less about people than their dreams.

After countless letters and phone calls, most of them unanswered, and interviews with dozens of potential informants, most of whom have no information, Harding does find his birth mother—along with two dozen half-siblings and cousins he never knew he had. The reunion with Maureen is moving but restrained: Harding displays an admirable resistance to mawkish scenes and above all to self-dramatization. He had worried about the distance they would need to travel: half a century of separation, and the deeper separation between the university-educated, middle-class son, and the mother who still lives in council housing.

Proceeding at first gently and tentatively, like dancers in rehearsal, he and Maureen get to know and like each other. Neither "blood" nor "nature" explains that affinity:

> What would blood prove if our meeting had turned out badly, as reunions can? Supposing Margaret had thought me a callow little prig who knew nothing about real life? If the blood-tie could bring love and loyalty to bear, it could also be an engine of bitter disappointment.

DOI: 10.1057/9781137333919

And for a moment, in a flash of intelligence I never quite regained, the process Margaret and I had begun turned into a second adoption. A two-way adoption without rules, of course, since either of us could pull out without prior warning, and at any point. But otherwise the similarity was striking. And if blood could go either way, then it wasn't the main consideration, any more than it was in old-fashioned infant adoption, where natural and social identities were reinvented in a single fluent movement.

What mattered was to want to engage with another person, and to continue believing this was a good thing to do. (p. 176)

The story ends well.

Notes

1   For perceptive readings of many of these texts, and others, see Marianne Novy, *Reading Adoption: Family and Difference in Fiction and Drama* (Ann Arbor, MI: The University of Michigan Press, 2005). The book includes a useful chapter on the Oedipus legend, mainly positioned in support of open adoption. Novy has also edited a volume called *Imagining Adoption: Essays on Literature and Culture* (Ann Arbor, MI: University of Michigan Press, 2001), which includes commentaries on both English and American writers.

2   Carol J. Singley, *Adopting America: Childhood, Kinship, and National Identity in Literature* (New York: Oxford University Press, 2011), p. 83.

3   William St. Clair, "But What Did We Actually Read?" *Times Literary Supplement* (May 12, 2006), pp. 13–15.

4   Joyce Carol Oates, *The Adoption, Conjunctions*, vol. 25 (fall, 1995), pp. 239–255.

5   Joyce Carol Oates, *Mudwoman* (New York: Ecco, 2012), pp. 79, 233.

6   P. D. James, *Innocent Blood* (New York: Charles Scribner's Sons, 1980), p. 14.

7   Ellen Ullman, *By Blood* (New York: Farrar, Straus and Giroux, 2012), pp. 167, 348.

8   Ellen Ullman, "My Secret Life," *New York Times* (January 2, 2009), A23.

9   Elie Wiesel, *The Sonderberg Case*, trans. Catherine Temerson (New York: Alfred A. Knopf, 2010), p. 165.

10   Aimee Phan, *We Should Never Meet* (New York: St. Martin's Press, 2004), p. 243.

11   Chang-rae Lee, *A Gesture Life* (New York: Riverhead Books, 1999), p. 1.

12   Elinor Lipman, *Then She Found Me* (New York: Washington Square Press, 1991), p. 1.

13   A. M. Homes, *The Mistress's Daughter* (New York: Viking, 2007), p. 7.

14   Jeannette Winterson, *Why Be Happy When You Could Be Normal?* (New York: Grove Press, 2011), pp. 1, 223.

DOI: 10.1057/9781137333919

15 Nancy Newton Verrier, *The Primal Wound: Understanding the Adopted Child* (Verrier Publications, 1993).

16 Jeremy Harding, *Mother Country: Memoir of an Adopted Boy* (New York: Verso, 2010 [2006]), p. vii.

DOI: 10.1057/9781137333919

Index

DOI: 10.1057/9781137333919

DOI: 10.1057/9781137333919

DOI: 10.1057/9781137333919

DOI: 10.1057/9781137333919

DOI: 10.1057/9781137333919

DOI: 10.1057/9781137333919

CPSIA information can be obtained at www.ICGtesting.com
Printed in the USA
LVOW13*1405111213

364868LV00005B/44/P